NIGHT
OF THE
SILVER
STARS

THE BATTLE OF LANG VEI

WILLIAM R. PHILLIPS

St. Martin's Paperbacks

NIGHT OF THE SILVER STARS

Copyright © 1997 by William R. Phillips.

Background image © Corbis
Silver star medal © Bettmann/Corbis

Library of Congress Catalog Card Number: 97-29824

ISBN: 0-312-99681-0

Printed in the United States of America

Naval Institute Press edition published 1997

St. Martin's Paperbacks edition / June 2004

St. Martin's Paperbacks are published by St. Martin's Press, 175 Fifth Avenue, New York, NY 10010.

10 9 8 7 6 5 4 3 2 1

This book is dedicated to those officers and men of the United States Special Forces who served at the Lang Vei Special Forces Camp when it fought for its life against a numerically superior force spearheaded by armor. Included in this dedication are those three Green Berets who were at the Old Lang Vei camp and performed counterassaults that were above and beyond the call of duty. The book is also dedicated to those MACV-SOG Special Forces of Forward Operating Base Three at Khe Sanh who formed the extraction force, as well as to their army and Marine Corps helicopter pilots. The survivors of the above-mentioned elite forces have expressed their desire that the book be further dedicated to the most noteworthy of all of their number: those who did not return.

Finally, there is one nonparticipant who also shares this dedication: the late Col. Fred O. Jackson, U.S. Army (Retired), the father-in-law of Paul R. Longgrear, who took the place of the father he never knew.

Contents

Foreword

During the Tet Offensive of 1968 and the months preceding, the eyes of the world were focused on one tiny combat base in Quang Tri province, the northernmost part of the I Corps Tactical Sector in South Vietnam. It was the Marine Corps combat base of Khe Sanh. Khe Sanh was so important to the U.S. military situation that it received my constant attention as commander, U.S. Military Assistance Command, Vietnam. Looking over my shoulder were not only my military superiors, such as my immediate superior, the commander in chief, Pacific, Adm. U.S. Grant "Oley" Sharp, in Honolulu, but also the Joint Chiefs of Staff of the armed forces of our country. In turn, the commander in chief, U.S. president Lyndon B. Johnson, was so interested in the anticipated battle for Khe Sanh that he had a scale model of the base built for his daily perusal. In addition, the news media of the world also focused on this tiny outpost manned by the fighting marines of the 26th Marine Regiment (Reinforced), commanded by Col. David E. Lownds.

However, there was a buffer to this seemingly

exposed six-thousand-man bastion: a little-known Special Forces camp some nine road miles closer to the Laotian border and the Ho Chi Minh Trail that had been specially built as a "fighting camp," manned by Team A-101 of the Green Berets, commanded by Capt. Frank C. Willoughby. Willoughby had selected the site for the camp and had overseen its construction; it replaced another Special Forces camp that had been overrun in early May 1967. The new camp became known, as most Special Forces camps were, by the name of the closest village, Lang Vei, the same name as the ill-fated camp before it.

The story of the Battle of Lang Vei is presented here in detail, with unswerving dedication to objectivity and accuracy by its author, former U.S. Marine 1st Lt. William R. Phillips, who served under my command from the time he landed with the third marine combat battalion to arrive in Vietnam in March 1965. He remained under my command until the end of his tour in February 1966. Phillips has a special interest in the battle, as he is alternate next of kin to a Green Beret who was listed as missing in action from the Battle of Lang Vei on 7 February 1968, Sp5c. Daniel R. Phillips.

The author has spent more than seven years researching and writing this study of a very important and very significant battle that could well have had an impact on the enemy's thinking about attacking Khe Sanh in force. Our artillery and air support, as well as the heroic defensive battle fought by two dozen Green Berets and several hundred indigenous troops that the Green Berets personally recruited and trained, is worthy of study by students of military history in general and of the Vietnam War in particular. Phillips has interviewed key personnel involved, from Capt. Allan Imes, who was an early commander of the Special Forces camp at Khe Sanh in 1964, to the Team A-101 commander, the executive officer, and the team sergeant during the Battle of Lang Vei, as well as the leader of the MIKE Force unit and a Special Forces medic sent to provide help. The extraction force from MACV-SOG was interviewed in depth.

But the interviews did not stop there. Wanting the perspective of the man who had been the 5th Special Forces Group commander prior to the battle, the author talked to Col. Frank "Blackjack" Kelly, who preceded Col. Jonathan Ladd, the commander during the battle. Phillips followed this with an interview of the man "on the ground," Khe Sanh's commander, Col. David E. Lownds. Phillips and I have discussed the decision by the marines not to send in the relief force, as well as my part in ordering marine aircraft to move the Green Berets from the SOG unit at Khe Sanh to rescue the survivors. I have had the opportunity to review the manuscript before publication and can only say that it appears to me that every conceivable effort to portray accurately the Battle of Lang Vei, and the extraction of its survivors, has been made by the author. I am pleased to recommend the book to those who wish to read of the valiant defense a small group of U.S. soldiers and attached indigenous troops put up against a numerically superior force of North Vietnamese Army troops led by armor in an assault for the first time in the Vietnam War.

William C. Westmoreland

Acknowledgments

I would like to express my warmest love and thanks to my best friend, roommate, and wife, Peggy Joyce Phillips, without whose support this book would never have been completed and who, in the company of a toddler named Kelley, suffered through twelve months of mental anguish while I served my tour in Vietnam from March 1965 to February 1966.

In August 1989 my son Randy bought me a book on the Vietnam War. In it were listed the missing in action. In reading through it, I happened upon the name of my first cousin, Daniel R. Phillips. After exhaustive research, aided by many strangers who became telephone friends, the story was put together. Early on, a reunion with Betsy Phillips Hallam provided a look into the past.

My children—Kelley, Randy, and Gretchen—were a collective source of inspiration and energy.

Dr. Mildred F. Wallace, author and longtime friend, persistently encouraged me, never tiring of pushing a sometimes resistant and obstinate marine to finish what he had started.

Dr. David Lu, retired chairman of the East Asian

Studies Department of Bucknell University in Lewisburg, Pennsylvania, read the manuscript and encouraged me to publish it, at a time when the project was almost dead.

Steve Sherman of Houston, Texas, a collector of information regarding the Special Forces, gave some initial assistance that led to contact with the Joint Casualty Resolution Center, commanded at the time by Lt. Col. James Cole. Cole and his successor, Lt. Col. Mack Brooks, were extremely helpful in gathering information on Lt. Daniel R. Phillips. The POW/MIA office of the Defense Intelligence Agency also was very helpful, through the efforts of Col. Joseph Schlatter and his successor, Col. Millard Peck.

Col. Joe Schlatter served as the speaker at the Milton Hershey School ceremony in which Betsy Phillips Hallam and I presented the medals awarded to Lt. Daniel Raymond Phillips, to be displayed in the school's rotunda. Mike Peck was a valuable sounding board in the early days of the manuscript.

The Green Beret who was an integral part of this effort from the beginning was Paul R. Longgrear, who commanded the MIKE Force at Lang Vei as a first lieutenant. I found Longgrear through information provided by the late retired Capt. Joseph A. McElroy, USMC. Paul was a bastion of information, hope, and support.

Retired Com. Sgt. Maj. William T. Craig, Team A-101's senior enlisted man, was a source of great encouragement and advice throughout the effort. Retired Maj. Frank C. Willoughby, the commanding officer of Team A-101, was a key player in the final edition of the manuscript and gave many hours of patient answers. Frank

Willoughby's review of the manuscript, and his sharing of personal photographs and information gleaned from a February 1995 visit to Lang Vei with the Joint Task Force for a Full Accounting, provided not only much material for the manuscript, but pictures and maps.

Miles Wilkins, first lieutenant and executive officer of Team A-101, provided his views on the battle and told of his harrowing escape and near-death experiences. Richard Allen, then a sergeant with the three-man medical team at Old Lang Vei, shared his memories of his thoughts and actions of twenty-eight years ago.

Jim Muchler and Doug Eaton of Bucknell University's Administrative Services Department deserve a pat on the back for their help with the book's artwork. Doug Eaton's computer-graphics skills transformed my futile attempts at drawing into quality illustrations.

Dr. Jack Shulimson of the History Writing Unit, Marine Corps Historical Center, shared his notes on Lang Vei with me, as did U.S. Army Military History Institute professionals John Slonaker, Thomas L. Hendrix, and David Keough. Roxanne M. Merritt, curator of the JFK Special Warfare Museum, was an early source of information.

Many other friends lent encouragement and support during seven years of research and writing. They are too numerous to list, but among them are George Humbert, Gregory Kirk, Donald Manning, Dennis Hopple, and George Waltman.

I was fortunate to make the acquaintance of one of our nation's foremost leaders of men in battle, retired Gen. William C. Westmoreland, whom I interviewed about his part in sending in the extraction force.

Mark Gatlin of the Naval Institute Press evidently saw possibilities, for which I will always be grateful. Gatlin was patient and understanding and became a friend, as did Gary Linderer, publisher of *Behind the Lines,* who made my Lang Vei story the lead article in the September–October 1996 issue of the magazine.

Prelude

This is the story of one of the most significant battles of the Vietnam War, or what some scholars call the Second Indochina War. The latter name is, in my humble opinion, more correct. The war did not stop at the borders of North and South Vietnam. It spilled over into the neighboring countries of Laos, Cambodia, and Thailand. Huge B-52 bombers took off daily to bomb North Vietnamese targets in Cambodia and Laos as well as in North Vietnam from as far away as Guam and Okinawa and from as close by as the enormous airdrome at U Tapao in Thailand. The Ho Chi Minh Trail, the major supply lifeline of the communists in South Vietnam, originated in North Vietnam and traversed through both Laos and Cambodia to many points along the South Vietnam border.

In a lot of ways it was a very strange war, fought by some very strange but interesting people, in ways that were extremely unconventional. Some of these unconventional players on our side were mercenaries, gunslingers for hire. A number of nationalities were included in this category, from U.S. Central Intelligence

Agency contract pilots who were usually American civilians to combat troops of Chinese extraction (Nungs), also reportedly in the pay of the CIA (Central Intelligence Agency).

In the mid-sixties, it was not uncommon for a platoon of Nungs to be commanded by an Australian staff noncommissioned officer with bush-warfare experience in Malaysia. The Nungs also provided security forces for selected American headquarters units of Special Forces. In addition they manned elite units, commanded by Green Berets, that acted as "hatchet" (quick-reaction) strike forces for the highly classified missions of the Military Assistance Command Vietnam, Studies and Observation Group (MACV-SOG).

Although they did not think of themselves as mercenaries, Cambodian troops composed the Mobile Guerrilla Force, trained and led by U.S. Special Forces to operate in enemy-controlled territory.

In addition to conventional American units, which included army, navy (including Naval Construction Battalions, or Seabees), air force, and marines, there were also unconventional units. The men in these unconventional units tended to be freewheeling, independent, fierce fighters who spent much of their time in "Indian Country," as that land beyond the outer-wire perimeter came to be called in American military encampments. Perhaps the most famous of these were the U.S. Special Forces, the Green Berets. They trained indigenous mountain tribesmen, called *moi*, or "savage," by the South Vietnamese, to be an effective fighting force. These montagnards, or mountain people, as the French christened them in the First Indochina War, primarily occupied combat outposts to interdict enemy movement into the South. The Green Berets maintained many small outposts far from the large bases that came into being after the first major combat units arrived in South Vietnam in March 1965.

Lang Vei was just such an outpost in late January 1968, at the time of the Tet Offensive. It was manned by about three hundred South Vietnamese and Bru montagnards of the Civilian Irregular Defense Group (CIDG), a Mobile Strike Force (MIKE Force) of nearly two hundred Hre tribesmen, three combat reconnaissance platoons (two of Bru tribesmen and one of South Vietnamese), thirteen Vietnamese Special Forces, and twenty-four Green Berets.

The strategic importance of Lang Vei was largely based upon its location. It adjoined Route 9, east of the Laotian border and the Ho Chi Minh Trail, west of the Marine Corps combat base at Khe Sanh. Lang Vei would be a deterrent to any massive enemy movement in the direction of Khe Sanh. Any analysis of the Battle of Lang Vei must include its role in the larger picture of Khe Sanh, anchor of defense in northernmost South Vietnam.

An integral part of the Battle of Lang Vei is specifically the story of four of the twenty-four Green Berets who came to be gathered in that one small camp on a momentous evening in February 1968. These four represent the other twenty: two officers, one senior enlisted man, and one "new guy." One officer, who commanded the A-Team, was responsible for the planning and building of the camp, as well as recruiting and training the CIDG. The second officer commanded the MIKE Force composed of Hre montagnards. The senior enlisted man was at the camp during most of its construction and had much experience in the Indochina theater, including Laos and Thailand. The new guy had been in Vietnam only three weeks and in the army only twenty-three months, but he was already a specialist fifth class, the fifth enlisted grade. Unfortunately, he would be one of the five men of the group still listed today on the granite wall at the Vietnam Memorial in Washington, D.C., as missing in action (MIA). He is the representative of those forgotten men that some authors have called "the men we left behind." He was not a pilot whose plane was last seen over the water, out of control. He was what was once called a Category 1 MIA: the enemy had certain knowledge of what had happened to him. He was in a unit overrun by North Vietnamese regulars, who were known to keep meticulous records of their prisoners.

These four men were as varied as could be imagined, yet they had certain characteristics in common. The senior commissioned officer, Capt. Frank C. Willoughby, was a tall, lanky, no-nonsense leader who had served as an enlisted man in the U.S. Marine Corps for four years before joining the U.S. Army as a private. The other commissioned officer, 1st Lt. Paul R. Longgrear, was a fun-loving, hell-raising former Arkansas State student whose life would be changed forever by his experience at Lang Vei. The old pro, Sfc. William T. Craig, was a Korean War veteran and one of the early members of the Special Forces. The new guy, Sp5c. Daniel R. Phillips, had arrived from the "real world" only three weeks earlier. Three of the four had much in common. All but Willoughby came from bro-ken homes. All but Willoughby were college dropouts. All had found a home in the U.S. Army's elite Special Forces.

The four would arrive at Lang Vei by different routes and at different times, but their common experience in a most ferocious battle would forever imprint itself on the remainder of their lives. Together they and their fellow Green Berets would put up such a fight that Gen. Vo Nguyen Giap must have had to revise his planning on the Khe Sanh marine combat base just over five air miles east on Route 9. In the annals of U.S. forces in combat, Lang Vei and its heroic defense must forever hold a place. It was one of the battles that made of the Green Berets a lasting symbol of their motto for com-bat: Any Time, Any Place.

The violent, deadly events that occurred that Febru-ary night and the next day resulted in one of the finest examples ever of collective bravery, endurance, and ut-ter will to survive in war. If medals for heroism are any measure of courage on the battlefield, then Lang Vei is a symbol for all time. Every one of the twenty-four Green Berets present during the battle earned at least one combat decoration. One received the Medal of Honor, the nation's highest award; one was awarded the Distinguished Service Cross; nineteen were hon-ored with the nation's third-highest award, the Silver Star; and three received the Bronze Star with Combat V for valor. Thus 6–7 February 1968 was truly the night of the Silver Stars.

Only two (including one MIA who was never seen again) were not wounded. Although relatively small numbers of U.S. troops were involved, the significance of the struggle will be clear to any reader. The event that took place was to be called, simply, the Battle of Lang Vei.

1
Boom City

The Geneva Accords of 1954 established a demilitarized zone (DMZ), a temporary imaginary boundary. In January 1968, it still divided the country into North and South Vietnam. North Vietnam was still trying to take South Vietnam by force, as it had been since 1959. The DMZ was north of the main road (Route 9) that traveled roughly east-west from the national highway, Route 1, which was even more roughly a north-south road near the coast.

Army and marine officers spend much training time, particularly as young second lieutenants, in terrain appreciation. They learn to select dominant terrain features, such as high points, that could effectively dominate a battle. In northernmost South Vietnam, in the province of Quang Tri, the Khe Sanh plateau is such a dominant feature. In military parlance, hills bear the names of their elevation. The Khe Sanh plateau boasts a number of these strategic hills. Most lie between two and five miles from what was in January 1968 the U.S. Marine Corps combat base near Khe Sanh. The military camps often usurped the village names, even though they might be several miles distant. Such was the case with Khe Sanh, and with its offspring, Lang Vei.

Before the arrival of a Green Beret A-Team on 8 July 1962, the Khe Sanh plateau was a lush, rich land, well-suited to the growth of coffee beans. There was abundant water, and the native Bru tribesmen were friendly to the European planters. The area had its share of important visitors between the First and Second World Wars, due to a ready supply of trophy animals that included tigers, bears, deer, and panthers. The Poilane family established a coffee plantation in the years just after the First World War. Route 9 provided access to Savannakhet, on the Sepone River in Laos, for the necessary market.

The coming of the Americans, preceded by the war in Laos, had cut off the use of Route 9, effectively in both directions, for the Khe Sanh planters. The Green Berets had taken over several old French bunkers north of Khe Sanh and Route 9 for a long-range patrol base. They immediately recruited and trained some of the Bru tribesmen to assist them. The Bru, one of South Vietnam's twenty-nine mountain tribes known as montagnards, formed part of the Civilian Irregular Defense Group, or CIDG, trained by the Special Forces. The mission of the Special Forces was to train and use the CIDG as eyes and ears that would provide a reliable source of intelligence information. The CIDG learned to defend themselves and their villages or hamlets in the event of attack by the Viet Cong. The Bru knew the terrain, and they would fight to defend their homes. They did not, however, care much for the government in Saigon, and the feeling was mutual in the capital city.

The French Expeditionary Forces had identified the Khe Sanh plateau and its military value in the early fifties. They built fortifications near Khe Sanh and Lao Bao on the Laotian border, less than ten air miles apart. The Special Forces contingent kept watch on the Laotian border, the DMZ, and Route 9. Obviously, this was a lot to ask from one A-Team and their Bru CIDG. The fertile soil and the key terrain features made the Khe Sanh plateau a valuable piece of real estate.

A new A-Team from the 7th Special Forces Group (Airborne) at Fort Bragg, North Carolina, arrived at Khe Sanh in December 1963 for a six-month tour of temporary duty. Capt. Floyd Thompson commanded the team. Some three months into his tour, Thompson's L-19 aircraft crashed when it was hit by antiaircraft fire north of Khe Sanh while on a reconnaissance mission. Although badly injured, Captain Thompson survived the crash and returned home in Operation Homecoming in March 1973, after nearly nine years as a POW.

The rotation of A-Teams at Khe Sanh continued, as did the buildup of the CIDG. Three Australian Special Air Services soldiers arrived at Khe Sanh. They helped the A-Team, now commanded by Capt. Allan Imes, in its border-patrol duties. Capt. Reginald Pollard, son of the Australian army's chief of staff, brought with him two sergeant majors, one of whom was George Chinn, who would become the senior sergeant major of the army. Even though Pollard was senior to Imes, the highly regarded Aussies were content to follow Imes. The CIA provided the protection of a platoon-sized contingent of Nung troops.

With the CIDG now numbering about five hundred,

the mission was still difficult due to the extremely thick foliage and steep incline of the hills. A day's patrol might cover only three hundred to four hundred yards. This would be important to remember in the event a relief force had to cover ground quickly in an emergency situation.

An Army of the Republic of Vietnam (ARVN) infantry battalion, advised by two Green Berets, took up a position at nearby Lang Vei, some eight miles west of Khe Sanh on Route 9. Although Route 9 continued west beyond Lang Vei to the Laotian border, mines planted by the Viet Cong greatly limited its use.

As summer began, Captain Imes received a U.S. Marine platoon (reinforced), plus a Marine Force Recon team. While standing orders prevented the marines from accompanying the Green Berets on combat patrols, there were a few exceptions. The marines, too, needed combat experience to improve their already considerable ability to fight.

The Viet Cong did not attack the patrols; instead they blew up all but one of the nine bridges between Khe Sanh and the coast. Captain Imes was no slouch when it came to planning. Because of Route 9's condition, the French planters now had no way to get their coffee beans to market. Imes utilized his supply aircraft to fly back, loaded with the planters' coffee beans instead of with an empty cargo compartment. This kept the money flowing in, and Captain Imes believed that the French planters paid the Viet Cong protection money. If the Viet Cong decided to let the planters alone, that was one problem he would not have to face, and he certainly had his hands full as it was.

The relative tranquillity of the plateau changed a bit after the incidents in the Gulf of Tonkin occurred in the summer of 1964, and their follow-up actions thereafter. Gen. John K. Waters, commander of the army forces in the Pacific theater, visited Khe Sanh to personally brief Imes regarding a potentially disastrous situation. Intelligence estimates placed upwards of twenty thousand North Vietnamese regulars massed just north of the DMZ. The best guess was that they would invade South Vietnam in response to the Tonkin Resolution. Obviously, it would not take that many North Vietnamese Army (NVA) soldiers long to simply overrun Imes's small unit. Imes had instructions to let his CIDG melt away at the first sign of attack. However his A-Team and marine recon team would stay behind, avoid capture, and conduct guerrilla actions against the NVA.

Before Imes's A-Team rotated back to the States in November 1964, a patrol led by the two senior Aussies, Captain Pollard and Sergeant Major Chinn, ran into an NVA company actually camped inside South Vietnam. The firefight that resulted was a victory for the patrol, but no convincing signs were found of the supposed enemy buildup.

The ensuing two years, 1965 and 1966, brought large numbers of U.S. combat troops to South Vietnam. Accompanying the buildup of forces came orders from the commanding general of MACV, Gen. William C. Westmoreland, to take the offensive. Westmoreland wanted to take an unconventional war and make it his idea of an American kind of war: U.S. superior weaponry and firepower whenever possible against the Viet Cong and NVA main-force units. That way he could envision the Americans and South Vietnamese and their allies as victors in the war of attrition. Westmoreland believed that it was necessary to kill the enemy faster than they could recruit and train. To accomplish this objective, he planned to use U.S. air superiority to destroy North Vietnam's industrial capacity and transportation and communications systems. He felt that this constant pressure would destroy their will to fight and their ability to win.

The 173d Airborne Brigade engaged in several key battles in 1967: Operation Junction City (which featured a battalion-sized paratroop drop), near the Cambodian border, and the fight at the Dak To Special Forces camp. There were other operations involving fairly large Marine Corps units as early as 1965. The Big Red One (1st Infantry Division) and the 25th Division joined in a large search-and-destroy mission in Operation Cedar Falls. These operations were leading up to what General Westmoreland really wanted: a face-to-face confrontation with division-sized communist forces. Westmoreland wanted to eliminate sizable enemy forces by getting them out in the open and pounding them with superior U.S. firepower.

General Westmoreland sent a marine battalion commanded by Lt. Col. Van D. "Ding Dong" Bell to the Khe Sanh area in April 1966. Well-known throughout the Corps for his toughness and readiness, Bell, looking for a fight, led his marines to an area controlled by a main-force NVA unit. He also intended to familiarize himself with the situation and the terrain, especially that of the western mountains. Because of bad weather, the marines had to delay their arrival at Khe Sanh for two weeks. Bell's battalion searched the area and even marched home on Route 9, trying to provoke an ambush. Unfortunately, nothing happened. The intense heat provided the only marine casualties, which their navy medical corpsmen had to treat.

Westmoreland, still not satisfied that all was well, ordered the runway, originally built by the French, extended. The marines disagreed with General Westmoreland, respectfully of course, on putting a battalion of their 26th Regiment in Khe Sanh. Their arguments were logical. The isolated location would require extensive effort to resupply it by air. The weather was bad enough to keep the C-130s from flying Bell's troops in for two weeks, so it, too, would be a negative factor. When General Westmoreland suggested putting the battalion in, the senior marine officers reminded him that it was not only Khe Sanh they would have to defend, but also the surrounding higher elevations. Apparently the marines, too, had studied the Battle of Dien Bien Phu.

However, in the military, rank has its privileges (RHIP). Even if General Westmoreland was wrong, he was the man calling the shots. Westmoreland had never been totally happy with his marines. He believed that they always underestimated the capabilities of the enemy. Westmoreland may have misunderstood Marine Corps confidence, the belief that the Leathernecks were the greatest fighting force in the world. In any case, there was friction between Westmoreland and the marines. Even so, the marines sent the requested battalion to Khe Sanh.

This did not sit well with the Green Berets. While

the A-Team had gotten along with their marine platoon and recon team quite well, when the marine battalion staff arrived, especially field grade officers (major and above), the situation changed. Marine officers do not like to see any fighting men unshaven or with hair long enough to comb. They considered the Special Forces to be ill-disciplined and unmilitary, and they certainly did not understand fully the role of the Green Berets.

The Green Berets immediately felt unwelcome, and they did not need harassment from officers of another service. They felt that the marines were fine for amphibious landings on hostile shores, but they did not feel that they could handle the clandestine long-range patrols behind enemy lines, nor the training and controlling of the montagnards. This job was what the Green Berets were famous for, and they did it as well as anyone. The marines did not like or trust the indigenous troops, and that situation would worsen before long. The marines had displaced the Green Berets from their French-built bunker at the airstrip, again using the RHIP factor. The Green Berets and their montagnards moved about eight road miles farther west on Route 9 to Lang Vei, a hamlet occupied by Bru tribesmen.

A most unfortunate incident occurred in the Bru hamlet of Lang Vei in January 1967. U.S. fighter bombers erroneously attacked the Bru hamlet with cluster bombs and high explosives. The Special Forces, located just across the road, tried in vain to find the radio frequency the planes were using, to no avail. It was a disaster. Over one hundred Bru tribesmen died in the attack.

It required months of supreme effort by the Green

Berets, including a special advisory team headed by Maj. James Whitenack, to undo the damage of the air attack on their Bru friends. The Bru were invaluable to the Green Berets, because they knew what the enemy was doing and would alert them to danger. Such was not the case in their relationship with the marines.

The marines proved to be correct in their firm conviction that they must control the surrounding hills. In late April 1967, the first of what became known as the Hill Fights began. Hill 881 South was the first target. Reinforcements, rushed to the scene, ran into an ambush. The Viet Cong used similar tactics to the Viet Minh before them. Strike and wait for the onrushing reinforcements, and ambush them. Then ambush both groups as they try to return to their base camp.

The dawn of a new day saw another marine battalion arrive at Khe Sanh. Before that day was over, the new battalion was up to its eyeballs in a firefight on Hill 861. Another new day brought another marine battalion, closely followed by an artillery battalion. It did not take the marines long to decide that their enemy was formidable: they were professional soldiers, not ill-trained and ill-equipped guerrillas. The marines soon found that they were up against NVA regulars, with extensive combat experience against the French.

Many of the young marines, although new at this deadly game of war, well used their excellent training, discipline, and motivation. The Hill Fights continued, but the NVA, like the Viet Cong, melted away quickly after the firefights. They were still not using the large main-force units that military intelligence felt were gathering nearby.

The NVA's 325-C Division had pulled its 18th Regiment, battered by the marines in the Hill Fights, back to Laos to refit. With this diversion, the NVA sent in its 95-C Regiment to hit the Green Beret camp. Team A-101, commanded by Capt. John J. Duffy, had moved into the position in late 1966. Inactivity in the area on the part of the enemy had led Duffy to utilize the services of the local Bru from the Lang Vei village to clear the unmarked minefield. Whoever ordered the minefield's removal outranked the A-Team commander, and that decision unnecessarily weakened the camp's defenses.

It was done against Duffy's better judgment, but his time had come for transfer. It would be his replacement, Capt. William A. Crenshaw, who would suffer the consequences of not listening to an experienced senior NCO. Sfc. Bill Steptoe was the team sergeant of A-101, and he returned from a week-long patrol on that third day of May 1967 to meet his new commander. Steptoe's thirty men had patrolled north of the DMZ, in one of those situations where the NVA were close enough behind them that they must have been able to smell the garlic on their collective breath. It had been touch and go for the patrol, who had survived several hairy situations and a nasty firefight that had kept them from being completely cut off and trapped.

Steptoe immediately took his concerns to his new boss upon his return to the camp. He recommended strongly to Captain Crenshaw that the camp go on full alert, as he was certain that an entire NVA division was hot on his heels and headed their way. Unfortunately, the A-Team commander rejected his advice. Crenshaw was a new guy, having been in country only two weeks and at the camp only a few days. Steptoe was getting a little tired of people not believing him. The marines had heard his patrol report of heavy enemy activity in divisional strength in close proximity, but the marines too had failed to give it any credibility. Crenshaw heeded the advice from his predecessor, Captain Duffy. Duffy had told him that there was no immediate threat from the enemy. He soon found out that his team sergeant's advice was sage. That night the enemy attacked the Special Forces camp at the original Lang Vei site, now known as Old Lang Vei, in force.

The camp's situation quickly became desperate when a Viet Cong platoon penetrated the defensive wire and, aided by an infiltrator and traitors within the CIDG, was soon attacking the command bunker. The company-sized force attacking the Lang Vei camp utilized support from mortars and, according to Francis J. Kelly in *U.S. Army Special Forces, 1961–1971*, the NVA tanks' main guns. The tanks did not attempt to penetrate the camp perimeter but remained in strictly a fire support role.

At approximately 0330 on 4 May, Maj. James Whitenack, the advisory-team commander in the village of Lang Vei, received a radio call from Bill Steptoe. Steptoe had stayed behind while his patrols were operating outside the compound. He had been asleep in the team bunker, as had been the soon-to-be-rotated executive officer, 1st Lt. Franklin D. Stallings, when the first rounds of incoming had hit at about three in the morning.

The two ran through rocket and mortar fire to the command bunker. Stallings, shot in the chest, never made it. Steptoe kept heading for the command bunker, but he was slightly wounded just as he reached the door. He quickly talked to Captain Crenshaw, with his back still to the door of the bunker. A burst from an AK-47 ripped through Steptoe's left shoulder and arm, at the same time killing Crenshaw.

Steptoe reported to Major Whitenack that the camp had come under heavy attack and that he believed that he was the only American still alive. Fire support from the marine artillery at the Khe Sanh combat base greatly assisted the CIDG defenders. At about 0500 the defenders finally repelled the enemy penetration, ending the attack.

Whitenack immediately set out with his small staff and arrived just as dawn was breaking. Major Whitenack's team found Steptoe near death. Fortunately, they also found two other Americans who had survived the cave-in of the roof of their communications bunker, which Steptoe thought had killed them. The two officers, Captain Crenshaw and Lieutenant Stallings, were the only Green Berets killed in action during the quick, vicious hit-and-run attack. Several other Green Berets were on patrol at the time. The after-action report listed five Green Berets wounded, seventeen CIDG killed and thirty-five wounded in the attack. Additionally, thirty-eight CIDG were missing in action. Reported enemy losses were seven killed and five wounded.

A Viet Cong had infiltrated the CIDG and helped immensely in the attack, as he related when captured after the battle. As ordered by the Viet Cong, he had recruited four of the CIDG to assist him.

The five had the complete layout of the camp,

including bunker locations, guard positions and strength, a sketch map, and even a knowledge of the supplies received from Khe Sanh. With intelligence as accurate as that, the Viet Cong knew exactly what they would encounter and were prepared down to the right place to exit after the attack. The infiltrator and one of the recruits had actually triggered the attack, killing two guards and guiding the NVA through the outer perimeter's barbed and concertina wire into the inner perimeter. Their actions had saved the enemy much time and loss of life. This infiltration could occur in any CIDG camp. Since there was really no way for military intelligence to clear all the CIDG recruits, there was no way to stop this very effective way of fighting.

When Capt. Frank Willoughby arrived at Company C headquarters in Da Nang in June 1967, he received a very short orientation to Vietnam, a four-hour briefing. His company commander, Lt. Col. Daniel Schungel, instructed him to head directly to Lang Vei. There he would decide whether to rehabilitate the overrun camp or establish a brand-new camp. For a man in country for only a matter of hours, this was a horrendous decision, but Frank Willoughby was no rookie. He had come from a tour as a company commander in Officer Candidate School at Fort Benning, Georgia, and he was recognized as a man of extraordinary military acumen. While at Fort Benning, Willoughby had had the distinct privilege of briefing the president of the United States, Lyndon B. Johnson.

Captain Willoughby thoroughly checked out the area around Lang Vei. His company commander had given him the authority, without his having seen any other A-Team camps, to design and build a brand-new camp, if that was his decision. He could place the camp anywhere he desired, within his assigned tactical area of responsibility (TAOR), as long as it was capable of reinforcement.

After a deliberate and careful study, Captain Willoughby selected a hilltop about half a mile west, closer still to the Laotian border. Although the enemy had penetrated the defense of the old camp, they had not destroyed it completely. Nevertheless, it lacked the observation and fields of fire that the new location offered. Frank Willoughby never knew that the NVA had used tanks in support of the attack on the former Lang Vei camp. In his study, Kelly does not relate the passing of information regarding the tank support. Also, the repair of the damaged wire was a job made only for a madman, since the wire was in the midst of unmapped minefields.

Shaped very much like a dog bone, the new Lang Vei Special Forces camp would be on a plateau that had excellent fields of fire and a clear view of the Laotian border and Route 9. The new, heavily fortified "fighting camp" evolved so that only one-third of its authorized strength could successfully defend it. This concept allowed two-thirds of its force to be free to conduct offensive operations against the Viet Cong and NVA. The size alone of the camp that the new concept called for ruled out the smaller Old Lang Vei camp, which could hold a maximum of two CIDG companies.

The mission of the Lang Vei camp was to secure and pacify the surrounding area, interdict enemy infiltration routes, collect and pass on intelligence, and conduct border-surveillance operations.

Capt. Frank Willoughby, the new commander, soon encountered a serious problem: his inability to patrol in depth (more than a short distance) to the camp's north, east, and west. The boundaries of his TAOR limited his ability to gain accurate intelligence information on enemy movements, and this would prove critical in the near future.

WHILE THE marines were the victors in the Hill Fights, they also discovered a weakness in the supposedly state-of-the-art American weaponry. The new M-16 rifle cost many lives when it jammed during firefights. Widely circulated but perhaps exaggerated reports described the bodies of young marines shot to death while trying to assemble three-piece cleaning rods to dislodge rounds jammed in the rifle chamber. Later extensive investigation proved that most of the blame rested on the powder in the rounds. Meanwhile, the marines returned to the higher-powered, more reliable 7.62mm M-14s, with their greater range and stopping power. Their heavier bullets were also better at maintaining direction through the lighter jungle vegetation than were the M-16 bullets. The M-16 received several modifications before it was ready to prove its mettle as a fast-firing 5.56mm weapon. While the M-14 hit with more force, the lighter 5.56mm tumbled and did more damage to the flesh surrounding and behind the entry wound.

Next, it became necessary to rebuild the Khe Sanh airstrip to withstand the landings of fully loaded C-130 aircraft. After removing the steel matting from the runway, engineers bedded it with crushed stone from a nearby quarry in August 1967. During the rebuilding period, General Westmoreland experimented with a parachute resupply method known as Low Altitude Parachute Extraction. Air-crewmen pushed pallets of supplies through the open rear doors while the plane roared down the runway at a very low altitude.

General Westmoreland wanted heavier firepower available to the Khe Sanh marines, so a convoy towing 175mm artillery pieces headed to the combat base via Route 9. These big guns could fire rounds all the way into NVA bases in Laos, if necessary. While the transport of the big guns does not sound like a difficult task, there were a number of destroyed bridges along the way. Hasty bridges were a necessity in order to provide passage. Approximately ten miles west of Thon Son Lam, also known as the Rockpile, Route 9 entered the mountains. There, engineers had built the road into the mountainside. Due to the terrain contour, the road doubled back on itself. Over half of the road was one lane, with pullover points to allow oncoming vehicles to pass. Much of the route was prime ambush territory.

Army fire bases at Camp Carroll and the Rockpile protected Khe Sanh with their tremendous fire support. On the negative side, any fire support from these two bases to Khe Sanh–area targets required extra propellant charges to propel the big projectiles their maximum range. This caused premature wear on the barrels of the big guns, in contrast to wear from firing at targets with shorter ranges, and perhaps shortened their life by one-third or one-half. Also, the accuracy suffered when the 175s had to reach out that far. Since there were only the two 175mm fire bases in that area, the possibility existed that Khe Sanh might not be able to immediately respond to a request for fire support. Khe Sanh clearly needed the big guns to offer counter-battery fire against the NVA 130mm and 152mm artillery pieces entrenched in the Gibraltar of Laos, Co Roc Mountain. Another reason for sending them was that they could bring massive destruction to the enemy forces found in strength by recon patrols in Laos.

The Rough Riders of the 3d Motor Transport Battalion, 3d Marine Division, towing the big guns, formed on 21 July 1967. More than eighty vehicles headed west to the mountains, with each mile of the way guarded by marines from a rifle company of the 3d Battalion, 3d Marine Regiment at Ca Lu. The 1st Battalion of the 26th Marines protected the final stage of the perilous journey.

Unfortunately for the marines, the enemy knew that they were coming. The 2d Platoon of Mike Company, 3d Battalion, 3d Marines, had covered some five kilometers along Route 9 from Ca Lu toward Khe Sanh, ahead of the Rough Riders. It was a quiet, routine matter until the point man saw an NVA soldier yielding to a call from nature, relieving himself just off the side of the road. Catching the enemy soldier in an extremely vulnerable moment, the point man opened fire.

The marine platoon immediately took fire from the high ground on one side of the road and from a tree line on the other. Mike Company's 2d Platoon returned fire, estimating that they were probably facing equal numbers. That initial estimate soon escalated into a battalion of NVA. The 2d Platoon was in some deep trouble. The rest of Mike Company, along with a chopper and gun truck in support, followed by two tanks, came to the rescue of the overmatched 2d Platoon.

As the marines disengaged, word of the ambush quickly reached their base at Ca Lu. Lt. Col. Robert C. Needham, commanding officer of the 3d Battalion, 3d Marine Regiment, 3d Marine Division (3/3), had just enough time to stop the Rough Riders. Ca Lu offered the only turnaround point before Khe Sanh. The following day 3/3 hit the ambush site in force, but all they found was evidence of a well-prepared ambush site that had been awaiting the convoy: 150 well-camouflaged ambush positions. Route 9, shut down for the duration, prevented the Khe Sanh defenders from ever receiving the 175mm guns.

As the summer of 1967 turned to fall, the relations between the Green Berets and the marines continued to deteriorate. This may sound typical of the rivalry between highly trained, elite troops that are vying for "bragging rights," but it was much more than that. While marines had a reputation as scroungers that could come up with equipment and supplies as well as occasional luxuries in the midst of a hellhole, the Green Berets were perhaps even better. The local timber was not the type that makes sturdy bunkers, being susceptible to termites and other mysterious local wood-boring insects. It was quite a sight for the Khe Sanh marines, watching low-flying helicopters carry 8-inch-by-8-inch beams directly over them en route to the new Lang Vei Green Beret camp.

With the help of navy Seabees, the Green Beret A-Team at Lang Vei was setting up a veritable fortress for themselves and their montagnard CIDG. They had not given up on the CIDG program because of the infiltration possibility (or perhaps probability). The Green Berets actually imported 8-inch-by-8-inch beams from outside Vietnam. Seabees constructed reinforced concrete bunkers, with generators and electric lights. While the marines at Khe Sanh poured fuel oil onto their sandbags in a futile effort to keep the rats away, the Green Berets concentrated on protection and some of the comforts of home. Tension between the marines and Green Berets continued to mount.

The marines also distrusted the top-secret Studies and Observation Group, formerly located just south of Route 9 in an old French fort. The men of SOG were Green Berets who were performing very highly classified and extremely dangerous missions outside South Vietnam. They worked out of their small base camp, which they named Fort Dix. When the SOG unit moved to the southwest corner of the combat base at Khe Sanh, the distrust was almost comical. The marines listened in on their radio transmissions, and finding out what the other "friendlies" were doing became a game of cat and mouse.

The Green Berets were just as unhappy with the marines. When the Green Berets went on patrols, they could not count on artillery support if needed, as they were often out of effective range of the guns. Instead, they relied on small, quiet teams that moved with the stealth they had first developed at Fort Bragg and other training sites, and then had perfected in the field in Indian Country.

Unfortunately, now they had to remain out of sight

or detection of the marines, as they accused the marines of calling in air strikes against anyone not identified as being a marine. Worse yet, the marine pilots would report map-grid coordinates of their locations "in the clear" over the planes' radios, in an effort to determine if they were in fact U.S. troops. The Green Berets reminded the marines that the NVA also possessed radios, and soldiers who spoke English and could read maps. It was not a good situation.

Before the end of October 1967, the reconstructed runway at Khe Sanh was complete. Stockpiles of supplies poured into Khe Sanh. The next month brought intelligence reports of NVA troop buildup. Sensors in the jungle along the Ho Chi Minh Trail detected increased movement. Even something so seemingly insignificant as elephant feces found along the Sepone River by a Special Forces patrol was a clear indicator of the presence of an NVA pack train. The use of elephants was a positive sign that the enemy was moving heavy weapons. When the montagnards started moving away from their border villages toward Khe Sanh and its protection, military intelligence was busy trying to assess the situation and the immediacy of its deterioration. Meanwhile, operations staff planned the response.

By the time General Westmoreland traveled to Washington to meet with President Johnson on 28 November 1967, the political situation had changed completely from that of the summer of 1964, when Congress had passed the Tonkin Gulf Resolution. Even that action was under scrutiny, as some thought that the United States was the aggressor and not the victim, as Congress had initially believed. Antiwar protests were commonplace and gathering steam. The pressure on Johnson was growing. Westmoreland had thoroughly studied the effect of Dien Bien Phu and realized full well the significance of that loss on the French will to fight. It was not hard to imagine that the North Vietnamese high command was looking for another Dien Bien Phu. One great bloody nose, no matter what the cost in dead NVA and Viet Cong, could well persuade the United States to end their stay in Southeast Asia.

The maps in General Westmoreland's headquarters showed every location of significant American and South Vietnamese units. As Westmoreland pored over them, he was trying to think like Gen. Vo Nguyen Giap, his counterpart in Hanoi. Where would Giap find another Dien Bien Phu? Giap had been in command during that terrible battle in 1954. At Dien Bien Phu, Giap had outgunned the French and eliminated possible reinforcement or escape by air. The similarities between the situation at Khe Sanh and Dien Bien Phu were in some ways remarkable.

By late 1967, Giap had to be looking at the isolated combat base of Khe Sanh as a likely target. Intelligence reports had reinforced this idea. Khe Sanh, like Dien Bien Phu, had an airstrip. Also, for all intents and purposes, resupply and reinforcement were possible only by air. The weather, like that at Dien Bien Phu, could cut down on the availability of that vital air support.

On 2 January 1968, a sentry dog sniffed the still evening air and bristled. His handler knew the reason immediately. There was movement outside the wire. The marine sentry sent for help as six men showed themselves, standing unconcernedly and conversing quietly as they observed the marine defenses. 2d Lt. Niles Buffington and a squad of marine grunts arrived on the scene and quickly sized up the situation. The six wore uniforms similar to those of marines. When challenged, one of them reached toward his pistol belt. That act brought the marines, who already had the six in their rifle sights, to decisive action. They killed five of the six instantly, but the sixth somehow crawled away. When the marines retrieved the bodies, they soon learned that the deceased were NVA regimental officers on a very bold reconnaissance mission.

Intelligence reports placed the NVA's 325-C Division some fifteen miles northwest of Khe Sanh. A backup force consisting of two regiments of the NVA 320th Division was south of the DMZ in a position to reinforce any attack. Intelligence radio-traffic monitors overheard the rough communist equivalent of a U.S. Army corps, a "front," headquarters. The front headquarters, located in Laos, would control three NVA divisions: the 325th-C, the 320th, and the 304th. Further intelligence reports mentioned a newly built road from the mountains of Laos, terminating within fifteen miles of Khe Sanh.

General Westmoreland had a dilemma on his hands. He wanted to attack NVA units in Laos. At the same time his intelligence staff was warning him of a huge enemy buildup that could indicate a major attack on his staging area at Khe Sanh. Westmoreland wanted to entice the enemy to attack Khe Sanh with that kind of main force. If that happened, he could bring his superior firepower to bear on a substantial target and achieve his objective of attrition against the enemy. He planned a massive air bombardment and placed the invasion on the back burner for a time. The code name chosen for the heavy bombing campaign was Niagara. While the air staff worked on Niagara, the already busy intelligence staff was trying to determine the NVA order of battle.

The marines had already fought units of the NVA 325-C Division in the Hill Fights, so they knew what a formidable foe they would face. Dien Bien Phu had seen the 304th Division as one of the major assault units, but that was nearly fourteen years before. Those two divisions would probably carry the brunt of the assault, with the 320th Division waiting in reserve to exploit any success. The 324th Division was not far away in Laos. Believed to be providing logistical support during the buildup period, it would most probably assist in the assault phase if required. With each division estimated at ten thousand men, the combined assault force could number forty thousand.

The more General Westmoreland heard of the buildup, the more he was spoiling for a classic, conventional showdown. He devoted his considerable intelligence capability to the Khe Sanh area. The marines there spent their time digging into the fine alluvial soil that had been to the disadvantage of the defenders of Dien Bien Phu. The soil would collapse if artillery rounds exploded on or near dirt walls.

One characteristic of crack troops is that they do not appreciate the defensive role, and they do not like to dig deep bunkers to hide in during an assault. They crave the offensive role, the product of their training. They abhor sitting and waiting, like turkeys in a pen waiting to have their heads chopped off and their feathers plucked in time for Thanksgiving dinner.

While they waited, the Khe Sanh marines sent out reconnaissance patrols to poke and probe in an effort to find the enemy. The enemy, though, had their own method of avoiding this form of detection. They had their own men posted as a human detection unit. Instead of making contact, their job was to observe the marine patrols and then melt quickly away to alert their units. Until the time was right, the NVA would disappear into the cover of the lush vegetation.

Col. David E. Lownds, the commander of the 26th Marine Regiment, was well aware of the absolute necessity of controlling the hilltops surrounding his Khe Sanh combat base. He knew about Dien Bien Phu. He also knew that he needed enough marines to successfully defend his positions, but not too many to be supplied by the air force. He felt certain that his troops would one day fight the battle that might be the key to the whole American effort in Vietnam. They could not afford to lose. They would not lose. Like many marine commanders before him, he had an impossible task. He knew Marine Corps history and tradition. He knew that his men were ready. He also knew that he had firepower available to him that included the big 175mm guns of the army fire base at Camp Carroll and the Rockpile, Thon Son Lam. In addition, he had some of the most advanced electronic detection devices available placed in the surrounding areas.

On 20 January 1968, Colonel Lownds received an intelligence gift that seemed too good to be true. That afternoon a disgruntled NVA first lieutenant surrendered to marines on the Khe Sanh perimeter. Lt. La Than Tonc was a veritable fount of information. He knew the NVA planned a full-scale attack on all of I Corps, including Khe Sanh. The first reaction of many men in the position of the marine colonel is that such intelligence must be a ruse. La Than Tonc had to be a plant by the NVA to divert the attention of the Americans, while the real attacks took place elsewhere in an altogether different time and fashion.

How could an air defense first lieutenant know the detailed plans of his army? Could Colonel Lownds afford to ignore this possibly legitimate and hence invaluable intelligence bonanza? Lownds acted immediately on the chance that the information was valid. The attacks would begin against two of the key hills as well as the main combat base at 0030. Once they had conquered Khe Sanh, the NVA would roll up the rest of the area all the way to Hue. Lownds immediately informed the Special Forces unit at Lang Vei of the possible pending assault, sending a messenger, Gy. Sgt. Max Friedlander, by helicopter. Unfortunately, Capt. Frank Willoughby was on R and R leave and was never told of the intelligence report.

Lownds also informed his immediate superior, 3d Marine Division commander Maj. Gen. Rathvon Tompkins, sending an officer by aircraft to Da Nang. He placed Khe Sanh combat base and its surrounding hilltop defenders on Red Alert. Marine Corps intelligence personnel had already corroborated much of what the defecting lieutenant said. It had to be fact. Major General Tompkins and his immediate superior, Lt. Gen. Robert Cushman, who commanded all the marines in

Vietnam, concurred with Colonel Lownds in his belief that the information was genuine. General Westmoreland, briefed by General Cushman, also agreed on the authenticity of the information. The coming attacks would provide no surprise, up the chain of command that ended with the president of the United States.

Interestingly enough in the light of future events, Lieutenant Tonc revealed that NVA artillery and perhaps tanks, neither one of which thus far used against Khe Sanh, would support the attacks. Tanks had never been used in the assault against U.S. troops in Vietnam. Another chilling revelation was that the 2 January incident involving the bold reconnaissance of the six NVA officers was more than it had appeared to be on the surface. Lurking within pistol range of the bodies of the fallen NVA as the marines searched them at first light the following morning had been a company of NVA. Had they been there just to observe the marine reaction to the bold act, or to ambush any sizable reconnaissance unit that probed beyond the bodies?

At exactly the time Lieutenant Tonc had revealed, the NVA attacked Hill 861. On the other hill mentioned, Hill 881 South, the entire night passed without incident. But it was touch and go on Hill 861. The marines had their hands full of NVA. The defense wavered, but in brutal hand-to-hand fighting the marines pushed back their attackers and restored the perimeter before the light of dawn. The NVA were no match for the bigger, stronger marines, who thrived on the close-in combat. The tenacity of the defenders prevailed, greatly supplemented by the supporting fires of their buddies on Hill 881 South, who had received no incoming.

It was almost 0530 before the combat base at Khe Sanh came under attack. One of the first incoming NVA rockets hit an underground ammunition dump. Colonel Lownds lost much of his supply of ammunition to one very well placed rocket. The secondary explosions touched off by the blast created havoc within the marine defenses. However, the promised infantry attack never followed the rocket preparation. The marines could not even respond to the rocket attack, as they had no weapons with the range to reach them. The effect of the failure to deliver the 175mm guns because of the ambush now had a telling effect on the marines' ability to retaliate in kind.

The loss of the ammo dump precipitated a decision by Lownds to withdraw his few marines from Khe Sanh village. It had taken a thousand rounds of artillery to stop another NVA attack on the village. The handful of marines assigned there on civic-action duty were now leading the defense by the South Vietnamese. Lownds had lost all but a small part of his ammunition supply due to the rocket attack and subsequent fires that morning. The marines were in a bind.

In a repeat of what had happened at Dien Bien Phu, the air force delivered only about 15 percent of the supplies needed to maintain the marines that day, 21 January. To put the issue in perspective, the ammunition destroyed amounted to almost 1,500 tons, and the total daily target for resupply of all types of beans, bandages, and bullets was only about 160 tons. With all the ammunition nearly gone, it would take a small miracle for Khe Sanh to survive. The NVA had either been incredibly lucky or incredibly good to damage the capacity of the marines to fight with one single rocket and its secondary effects.

The twenty-first of January 1968 had been a tough day for the marines at Khe Sanh. It had also been a trying day for their commanders all the way up the line to the president himself. The words *Dien Bien Phu* appeared everywhere. The NVA had certainly gotten the attention of the American high command.

In the White House, President Johnson was nearly paranoid with the thoughts of those brave young American boys being overrun by hordes of screaming Orientals. He had already seen enough aluminum coffins wrapped in the red, white, and blue American flags. He would see more of them. The Tet Offensive was at hand.

2

A Spooky Place to Die

Lang Vei, the northernmost and perhaps the most isolated of Vietnam's sixty-four Special Forces camps, was especially noteworthy for the quality of reinforced concrete construction of its bunkers. It was less than a mile from the Laotian border, much closer than the nine road miles and perhaps five air miles from the combat base at Khe Sanh. The navy Seabees, specifically Mobile Construction Battalion 7, built the fortress at Lang Vei. The famed marine Rough Rider truck convoys reportedly delivered two of their last hauls to the new camp on 1–2 August, carrying construction supplies of lumber and heavy concrete from Dong Ha via Route 9. But Capt. Frank Willoughby disagrees. Willoughby cites the knocked-out bridges along the route as the reason the truck deliveries did not occur. The air force air-dropped seventy tons of construction equipment and supplies.

An enemy attack severely damaged the Old Lang Vei camp on the night of 3–4 May 1967. Construction of the new camp began almost immediately after Captain Willoughby had selected the site. By early September, the new compound sported the outside heavily reinforced concrete shell of its sturdy Tactical Operations Center (TOC), the majority of which was underground. The walls of the reinforced concrete bunkers were eight inches thick, including those of the fighting bunkers of all four CIDG companies. Sky Crane CH-54 helicopters, which look very similar to praying mantises, flew in the TOC's nine-inch-thick concrete ceiling, prefabricated in Da Nang.

As the TOC neared completion, the slabs arrived at the campsite. The Seabees had only to slide off one of them at a time on a front-end loader, set it into place, and then insert the next interlocking piece of the fortress's nearly impregnable top. Captain Willoughby disagrees with the official report of construction that shows a layer of unperforated PSP (perforated steel plate) covered by four inches of poured concrete. The only steel used, according to him, was in the concrete's reinforcing rods. Initial plans had called for twelve-inch-by-twelve-inch joists supported by like-sized posts to support the all-important roof of the TOC.

When Capt. Frank Willoughby had selected the site for the new camp, he had not been aware of the biggest problem he would encounter in its construction: land mines. The French had planted between thirteen and fourteen hundred mines, including .Russian and Chinese types in addition to their own. Additionally, several hundred Japanese mines dotted the area, an unwelcome reminder of World War II. The removal of the mines was a time-consuming, dangerous task. However, their presence showed Captain Willoughby that at least two other armies, the French and the Japanese, had shared his opinion of the tactical importance of the "New Lang Vei" camp.

Captain Willoughby relates an amusing event that occurred during the summer of 1967, during the initial stages of construction of the camp. It was mid-afternoon when the members of the A-team heard the sound of a single-engine propeller-driven aircraft headed east toward them. It was not a friendly aircraft, but it did attract their attention, because it was a two-seater biplane. A popular song of the day told the story of the cartoon character Snoopy and the Red Baron. The biplane performed a figure-eight maneuver over the camp. The pilot, barely visible in the rear seat except for what appeared to be a white, flowing scarf around his neck, tilted the plane slightly and dropped several 82mm mortar rounds. None exploded. The Green Berets cheered this act of bravado, World War I–style.

Several days later, men on watch heard the sound of the single-engine biplane again, flying east from Laos over Route 9. Someone yelled, "Here comes Snoopy!" The Green Berets quickly gathered near the TOC to see the same spectacle repeated. Again, none of the dropped mortar rounds exploded, but the camp had experienced the first known air attacks by the NVA.

DURING THE construction period, in late September, an ARVN battalion was heli-lifted into an LZ (landing zone) near the new camp. Two consecutive MIKE Force exercises west and south of the site protected the early occupation of the unfinished camp from 25 October to

14 November 1967. The new inhabitants, Special Forces Team A-101 along with their CIDG companies and a handful of Vietnamese Special Forces, moved into their new home during construction. The official relocation was complete as of 21 September 1967. Before the Seabees arrived, the A-Team had obtained an Allis Chalmers bulldozer, about the same size as a D-4 Caterpillar. It was inoperable for a period, but Sgt. Richard D. Mullowney, a member of Team A-101 for several months of the new camp's construction period, was one of those people who can fix almost anything mechanical. He got the Allis Chalmers running again and drove it all over the camp, doing those little projects that are necessary but not glamorous, such as digging a trash pit. Mullowney transferred just before Christmas to the "super spook" MACV-SOG unit at Forward Operating Base Three.

By the end of January 1968, just before the Tet Offensive, the Lang Vei Special Forces camp had seen some personnel changes. Capt. Frank Willoughby, a former marine NCO who had been on site since June, still commanded the A-Team. His team sergeant, Sfc. William T. Craig, arrived in September. Anyone who has ever served in the military knows that the commanding officer is in the position of highest responsibility. However, the senior NCO is actually the one who oversees the vast majority of the operations aspects on a day-to-day basis. This is not to suggest anything negative about the actions or experience of the commanding officers, including Captain Willoughby, but simply to set the record straight for the non-veteran reader. However, Frank Willoughby was an exception to that generality.

Willoughby had served in the U.S. Marine Corps from April 1956 until his honorable discharge as a corporal in April 1960. When Willoughby took over the A-Team, the word that he was a former "jarhead" (marine) spread through the marine combat base at Khe Sanh like cheap beer through the kidneys. Willoughby, one of eight children who had known hard times growing up, did not readjust well to civilian life. In June 1961, just two months too late to reenlist and keep his rank, Willoughby enlisted in the U.S. Army as a buck private and started all over again.

Frank Willoughby applied for Officer Candidate School (OCS), at the insistence of 1st Lt. Karl F. Schmidt, his B Company commander. At the time, Willoughby was a specialist fourth class serving with the 54th Engineer Battalion in Wildflecken, Germany. Schmidt had previously promoted Willoughby to acting sergeant for duty as the unit motor sergeant. In order for Willoughby to apply for OCS, he successfully completed an army-level Non-Commissioned Officers Academy. After appearing before battalion-, brigade-, and corps-level boards in the peacetime selection process, Willoughby attended and graduated from the premier Seventh Army NCO Academy, with honors. While attending the academy at Bad Tolz, Germany, he became acquainted with members of the 10th Special Forces Group (Airborne). It was through these friendships that Frank Willoughby decided that his ultimate goal would be to join the Special Forces.

Willoughby was one of only two candidates selected from a field of twenty-one applicants to attend OCS. By the fall of 1963, he had completed OCS and Airborne

School. He commanded 50th Officer Candidate Company, which, by lineage, was the original Officer Candidate Company in the U.S. Army. In April 1967, he graduated from Special Forces Officer Qualification School, ranked eleventh in a class of 140. One of his classmates was Lt. Paul Longgrear. Standing three inches over six feet tall, with reddish brown hair that topped a lean frame of 185 pounds, Willoughby was the recruiting-poster Special Forces officer.

When Captain Willoughby first arrived at the site of the New Lang Vei camp in June 1967 to begin construction, the morale of the CIDG troops was very low. The major montagnard tribe in Willoughby's TAOR for the Lang Vei camp was the Bru, and, on the whole, they were not unfriendly to the Saigon government, but rather indifferent. Many of the families of the Bru CIDG, physically the smallest of the montagnards, lived far away from the Lang Vei camp. To the Bru, the term *far away* meant anything more distant than a day's walk. The Bru were scattered from Lang Vei west into Laos and from Khe Sanh north to above the DMZ, as far as the Chinese border. Some of their families were too far away for them to visit. Their life expectancy was about thirty-five to forty years, and they chewed both red and black betel nut. As a result, their teeth turned the color of their preferred nut.

The main weapon of the Bru before the coming of the Green Berets had been the crossbow. They practiced the animist religion, worshipping the sun, moon, and stars, as well as the wind and the clouds. The wind's effect on cloud patterns could determine whether or not they would leave their huts. A pregnant woman ready to deliver had to leave the village and go into the jungle. She could only return with a healthy baby. If the baby was sick or deformed, she left it in the jungle and returned to her home. The men averaged about five feet in height, with the women even shorter. Typical Bru clothing included a loincloth for the men, and the bare-chested women wore a garment similar to a sarong. The Bru had suffered much during the war, and the best intelligence estimates that Captain Willoughby could obtain placed their number at between twenty-five and thirty thousand.

The first several days of June 1967 saw the Bru moved into Lang Vei village and into the smaller village just northeast of it. As part of the Strategic Hamlet Program, the South Vietnamese government destroyed many hamlets and moved their citizens into protected areas. One of those destroyed was Lang Troai, which lay to the south of the New Lang Vei camp then under construction. In their new locale, the Bru were clothed and fed. Because of the successful agricultural programs, the Bru soon became self-sustained to a degree, no longer solely dependent upon handouts. The change in their attitude was apparent as early as October.

The Vietnamese generally came from the coastal area east of Khe Sanh, some from as far away as Hue and Phu Bai. They had the same loneliness problems as did the Bru, whom they naturally looked down upon. Captain Willoughby learned early on why the Viet Cong could make inroads with the indigenous personnel. It was a simple matter of survival. One Bru district chief told him, "You Americans here for one year, then go home." The district chief presented Captain Willoughby with two important gifts: Frank and Jesse, his two Bru bodyguards, named after the infamous outlaw James brothers of the American West. Another little-known gift from the district chief, one for which Captain Willoughby had no desire or use, was his two tiny daughters, to be Willoughby's wives. The older was about ten, the younger about seven years of age. The older child barely reached Willoughby's waist. Gathering all the statesmanship that he could muster, Willoughby politely refused to take the girls to his camp. He somehow persuaded the chief, without insulting him, to raise them in good health. But Willoughby disappointed the chief by not taking the girls to the camp with him.

Captain Willoughby was largely responsible for recruiting the Bru tribesmen and was also very greatly respected by these primitive people. Willoughby trained them, fed them, and looked after them as if they were his own A-Team. There was one problem with the intense loyalty that the Bru showed for Willoughby: they refused to go on operations unless he was with them. There was a very good reason that the Bru felt attached to Willoughby. One evening in the late summer, the captain was taking one of his Bru CRPs (combat reconnaissance platoons) on an ambush near Lang Troai, south of the Lang Vei camp.

The ambush brought contact and a brief firefight. Willoughby pulled the Bru back about one hundred meters to regroup and count noses. Much like in the biblical parable of the lost sheep, one of the Bru was missing. Leaving the others, Willoughby returned alone to the scene of the firefight. On the ground lay the wounded Bru, not making a sound. Willoughby reached down and gently placed him over his shoulder, being careful to cause as little pain as possible to the Bru's leg wound. Willoughby received his first Bronze Star with a Combat V for Valor in that action, plus the undying admiration of the Bru.

Another problem that Willoughby had with his Bru soldiers was getting them to wear shoes. Their feet seemed better adapted to swimming than to walking, as they were nearly as wide as they were long. Willoughby estimates that over 90 percent of them went barefoot. The Bru men, used to wearing loinclothes, disliked trousers.

One incident stands out in Willoughby's memory regarding the first CIDG resupply mission at the New Lang Vei camp. A twin-engine C-123 aircraft came in low. A full-grown water buffalo with a parachute strapped around him dropped out the back door. A large crate of pigs followed. The Bru immediately slaughtered the water buffalo when it hit the ground. "Unfortunately," says Willoughby, "the air force and Special Forces never developed a crate that would stay together once it hit the ground. The crate would shatter, and there were pigs in the wire and running all over the place, twenty-five to thirty pigs being chased by the Bru." Willoughby still laughs at the thought.

SERGEANT FIRST Class Craig would one day retire as a command sergeant major, the highest enlisted rank. He served twelve years and two months in Special Forces, with ten consecutive years of overseas assignments from

September 1961 to October 1971. By the time he inherited the A-Team at Lang Vei in September 1967, he had already served two six-month temporary duty tours in Laos and three in Vietnam.

Born the son of a career army enlisted man at Fort Sill, Oklahoma, on a cold and blustery day in November 1926, Craig began life with a harelip and cleft palate. The birth defect required at least a dozen operations over an eighteen-month period to correct. Army life for a junior enlisted man's family in those days and in the Depression days that soon followed was hardship. A caste system that was the name of the game in the pre–World War II military compounded the family's difficulties. An enlisted man's wife and children had to endure being treated as inferiors, a position that their husband and father lived with every day. Craig grew up with a distinct dislike for the military in general and for officers in particular. He did not appreciate being looked down upon by officers' kids.

With the visible scars from the many operations he had endured, young Craig had been subjected to much ridicule. It followed that he became as good a street fighter as singer Johnny Cash's "Boy Named Sue." A good athlete who would rather compete in sports than studies, Craig entered Oklahoma A & M in the fall semester of 1945. In 1946 he transferred to Eastern Junior College, where he played basketball and baseball. A semester at a four-year college, Eastern New Mexico, followed. Eastern's coach had used his influence to help Craig obtain an athletic scholarship. Unfortunately, he tore cartilage in his knee. Surgery immediately repaired the tear in the summer of 1949, but

Craig's knee did not heal in time for the basketball season. A sorely disappointed Bill Craig saw his scholarship terminated at the end of the first semester.

Disgusted with school, he thumbed his way to booming Alaska and worked in construction until 3 July 1950, when he received a telegram. "Greetings!" it began. His hometown draft board in Comanche County, Oklahoma, had given Craig the distinction of being one of the first twenty-five draftees from the county for the Korean War. After a bus ride to Oklahoma City, all but one passed their physicals and received orders to sit tight at home and wait for further instructions within the next thirty days.

The draftees had specific instructions not to join any unit of the regular armed forces, National Guard, or reserves during that thirty-day period. William T. Craig nevertheless enlisted in the Thunderbirds, Oklahoma's own 45th Infantry Division. The Thunderbirds' tour of active duty began on 1 September 1950. Craig saw considerable action, including some ad hoc ranger training the hard way, behind enemy lines in Korea, led by a former ranger friend of his. The ranger gave his men, who numbered less than twenty, a week's training in small-unit tactics before leading them behind enemy lines for reconnaissance purposes.

At times the unit had to shoot its way back to its own lines. Trained as a combat engineer, Craig used his demolitions experience in some other tedious tasks, such as removing or destroying enemy mines. He had another unforgettable experience that many combat veterans have nightmares about many years later: his first combat kill, where he actually saw his adversary die.

In March 1952, Craig was with the recon unit ahead of the observation post (OP). The unit formed a line along a riverbed in the darkness, when a figure walked toward Craig's position. As the man bent over to speak, his heavy garlic breath alerted Craig. A burst of automatic fire from Craig's M-2 carbine silenced the first words of Mandarin. There was no time to ponder the situation as the entire unit opened up on an approaching squad of Chinese.

The report of the incident to higher headquarters revealed that the recon unit had saved the OP from being overrun by a reinforced company of Chinese. The recon unit had killed over sixty Chinese from the 607th Field Army. Bill Craig also received word of his promotion to sergeant first class (then E-6) that day. He assumed the responsibility of platoon sergeant for the incumbent, whose tour of duty had ended. The promotion brought a temporary halt to Craig's "snoop and poop" recon days.

His unit rotated back to the States by 6 June 1952. The Oklahoma National Guard's 45th Infantry Division had reason to be proud. Upon its return, the division deactivated from federal service and returned to the control of the National Guard of the Sooner state. Sfc. William T. Craig would soon be a civilian again. His hometown Lawton police force and barroom bouncers should have received fair warning of this happening.

After two years of barroom brawling and a number of arrests, on 12 March 1954 William T. Craig, civilian, did something that he had sworn he would never do. He reenlisted for four years in the United States Army as a corporal. He lost his sergeant first class stripes because he had more than one year's break in service. The main attraction for the Korean War veteran was a promised chance at what he really craved: airborne training. Unfortunately, the airborne training that the recruiter promised him would occur in a month would not happen for four years. He was the victim of an automobile accident that would disqualify him in the jump physical for many, many months.

Following a thirty-month tour of duty in tropical Panama, Craig finally passed the physical examination and airborne physical training requirement. He signed away eighteen months of his life, conditional upon achieving jump status after satisfactory completion of parachute training at Fort Campbell, Kentucky. As a proud member of the 101st Airborne Division's Screaming Eagles' 326th Combat Engineer Battalion, William T. Craig was thirty-two years old when he completed jump school. As was the practice at that time, Craig went immediately on to become a jump-master.

When his enlistment contract had only six months remaining, the unit recruiting NCO dangled a new and exciting possibility in front of him. Special Forces was recruiting, and Bill Craig easily met the qualification requirements. Special Forces appealed to fighting Bill Craig, the scrapper from Lawton, Oklahoma. They were field soldiers and challenged even the toughest paratroopers. For Craig, the deal looked good: a three-year reenlistment if he made the grade.

Bill Craig was one of 240 authorized NCOs that Special Forces added to its two existing units in September 1959. At that time, the 1st Special Forces Group (Airborne), the Far Eastern theater contingent based in Okinawa, had 200 Green Berets. The 10th SFGA, based in Europe, had an approximately equal number. Craig joined the 77th SFGA in early October 1959 at Fort Bragg, North Carolina, also the home of the famed 82d Airborne Division. The 82d and Craig's former division, the 101st, would supply most of the candidates for the new unit, which began training in early November 1959.

On 3 June 1960, Craig completed his training and was Special Forces qualified. Three days later the proud new SF troopers participated in a D-Day anniversary parade that also retired the colors of the 77th Special Forces Group (Airborne) and activated the 7th Special Forces Group (Airborne). Bill Craig's new Company A commander was a man who would one day become a Special Forces legend: then-Lt. Col. Arthur D. "Bull" Simons.

Team A-101 was fortunate to have Sfc. William T. Craig as its senior enlisted man. He was truly a valuable man to have around. One valuable lesson he learned, and it became crucial in the upcoming battle, was that bunkers are for sleeping. A man in a bunker may have some protection, but the tradeoff for zero mobility once a firefight begins may not be worth it. Once the artillery, rocket, or mortar preparation is over and the infantry assault begins, a soldier is much better off in a foxhole or trench. He can leave either of them in a hurry for a counterattack or movement to another position.

THE REST of the team, designated A-101, consisted of the executive officer, 1st Lt. Miles Wilkins, who reported to the team in August 1967, surprised to find that his team commander had been his Officer Candidate School company commander; the psychological operations and civil affairs officer, 1st Lt. "Beetle" Bailey; Sfc. James Holt, a medic; Sfc. Kenneth Hanna, a weapons specialist; S.Sgt. Peter Tiroch, an intelligence specialist; S.Sgts. Emanuel E. Phillips and Dennis Thompson, radio operators; S.Sgt. Arthur Brooks, a weapons specialist; Sgt. Nickolas Fragos, a medic; Sp4c. William G. McMurry, a radio operator; Sp4c. Franklin H. Dooms, a radio operator; and the newest member of the A-Team, a twenty-three-year-old specialist fifth class from Philadelphia, Daniel Raymond Phillips.

After completing one year at Harrisburg Junior College in Pennsylvania, Phillips had transferred down the road a few miles to Millersville State University. After three semesters, he had exhausted his savings and decided to return to Harrisburg to work full-time and again accumulate some funds for the completion of college. But by this time the United States was in a rapid troop buildup in Vietnam. It was where the action was.

On 18 March 1966, Phillips enlisted in the U.S. Army in Harrisburg. As part of his three-year enlistment contract, the army guaranteed him a chance to become an airborne soldier. At five feet seven inches, his 135 pounds was solid and would soon be fine-tuned muscle. Basic training has a way of accomplishing that sort of thing.

Everyone who has served in the military remembers two days—the day they enlisted and the day they were discharged. Also, if they were army or Marine Corps enlistees, they remember vividly the culture shock of getting off the bus. Waiting most impatiently for them was a man who seemed to be the size of Smokey the Bear, wearing the campaign hat that he undoubtedly had removed from Smokey's head in a most forceful manner. This fearsome figure bore the title "drill instructor," since more appropriate terms might frighten off many recruits before they had signed their names on the enlistment contracts.

It takes the drill instructor and his lethal-looking playmates approximately sixty seconds to terrorize unsuspecting recruits into a nearly catatonic state. Some cannot remember their names, others cannot hope to differentiate their right from their left in a consistently correct manner, still others feel a warm sensation trickling down the inside of their trouser legs. When the country is not at war, drill instructors have perhaps twelve or thirteen weeks to turn a bunch of undisciplined civilians into what are at least basically trained soldiers or marines. Basic training prepares the recruits for further advanced training hopefully before they are sent in harm's way.

In time of war, it sometimes becomes necessary to shorten this basic-training period to six or eight weeks, perhaps even fewer. The time frame depends upon the "meat-grinder count," the number of casualties already suffered by U.S. combat troops.

Just six days from the date of his enlistment, Dan Phillips began formal training as an army recruit in Fort Benning, Georgia. Phillips quickly learned the benefit of following orders as soon as he received them. Recruiters stress the wonderful things that the army offers a young citizen—be all that you can be.

Unfortunately, sometimes that means being as miserable as you can be. The sadists who make up military training schedules seem to arrange for pleasant weather while the recruits are in the classroom learning military courtesy and discipline. As soon as the thunder claps or the cold wind blows through the crack under the door, it is time for outdoor "fun" activities.

There is a reason for close order drill. The modern soldier may not go into battle in the manner of his predecessors, but when the bullets buzz by like so many maddened hornets and the man in charge says, "Hold your fire," you hold your fire until his command. You must also know that same discipline applies to every man with you.

Training breeds discipline, and discipline under fire is what wins battles. The best fighting men train until they can perform their duties in their sleep. There are many times in combat when everything becomes instant chaos, instant insanity. Anyone with half a brain is scared. The important thing is what the soldier does when he is scared half out of his wits. He reacts. Training, when done properly and repeated until ingrained in the brain, becomes reaction.

But basic training only teaches the rudiments of what the soldier must know to survive on the battlefield. Phillips arrived on 6 June 1966 at Advanced Individual Training, where he learned the finer skills of combat. His new home for eight weeks would be Fort Gordon, Georgia, home of the 3d Training Brigade. Phillips joined a group of other soldiers destined for eventual airborne training.

On 10 June 1966, Phillips volunteered for Special

Forces training. Upon acceptance, he agreed to undergo training in any military occupational specialty, as required by the needs of Special Forces. In so doing, he also volunteered for airborne training. Two months later, after mastering added combat skills, Dan Phillips was where he wanted to be—jump school.

It requires a special breed of person to jump from an airplane, suspended from a nylon parachute, fighting winds and pressure variants, perhaps through a hail of small-arms fire. The jumper must land on hostile ground, shed the chute that attempts to drag him away, and run to the rallying point to begin the tough part of the mission.

It is no wonder that soldiers without airborne training (called "legs" because of their primary mode of transportation) gaze with envy at the jump wings of an airborne soldier. It is a badge of accomplishment, a proof of courage. It is also a fact that there is only a one-letter difference between *guts* and *nuts*.

When Phillips's A-Team mentor, Bill Craig, made his fifth and qualifying jump, he was ecstatic. Maj. Gen. William Westmoreland, commanding the 101st Airborne Screaming Eagles, congratulated each of his 297 graduates that day in the early summer of 1959. Each received a handshake and a check from their Uncle Sam, their first month's jump pay. The commanding officer of the only combat jump in the Korean War had come a long way already, but he still had a long way to go on the road to chief of staff. Bill Craig also had a distance to travel in his army life. At that time, all of the Screaming Eagles' NCOs and officers were, upon successful completion of jump school, immediately sent on to jump-master school. Less than half of those beginning the even more demanding training failed. Bill Craig was among the 40 percent of his jump-master class to graduate.

Dan Phillips successfully completed his jump training at Fort Benning on 31 August 1966. On 1 September he reported to the U.S. Army Special Forces Training Group (Airborne) at Fort Bragg, North Carolina, to begin his quest for the Green Beret. His initial task was basic engineer training with a specialty in demolitions, another rather challenging test of the nervous system. On 27 February 1967, Phillips completed the twenty-three-week course in combat engineering and had his occupational specialty changed from light infantryman to demolitions expert. On that day he also received the coveted Green Beret as a qualified member of Special Forces. Now it was time for more practice before the big "final exam"—survival and success on the field of battle.

Time in garrison can be boring when a soldier knows that his comrades in arms are already facing death on a daily basis in some faraway land. Elite troops have always had trouble adjusting to the humdrum of peacetime, and towns bordering the military posts of elite troops often are victims of pent-up anxieties and emotions released by a few rounds of cheer in the local bars.

With the continued buildup in Vietnam and the Southeast Asia theater, more and more Green Berets went off to war. Some returned after performing missions that remain highly classified to this day. Others had to be content to practice their art in other areas, including training exercises in the back country of the United States.

One such exercise nearly ended the military career of Daniel Phillips. He suffered an injury while making a parachute jump near Missoula, Montana, on 9 August 1967. He remained in the local civilian hospital for five days, with contusions of the right cerebral hemisphere and lumbar spine. After additional treatment in Womack Army Hospital, he eventually was able to return to full duty.

Phillips received his orders on 14 November 1967, requiring him to report to Fort Lewis, Washington, for transportation to 5th Special Forces Group (Airborne), 1st Special Forces, Vietnam, by 12 January 1968. Promoted to specialist fifth class on 13 October, Phillips had received waivers, since he lacked sufficient time both as a specialist fourth class and in time served on active duty to qualify. He went to Philadelphia to spend that last furlough with his mother. Still single, he asked her to give any medals he might earn to his high school alma mater, the Milton Hershey School, in Hershey, Pennsylvania, if he failed to return. He was not unique in this preparation: every soldier headed for certain combat has premonitions of impending death.

Phillips reported to Headquarters, 5th Special Forces Group (Airborne), 1st Special Forces, in Nha Trang, Vietnam, on 15 January 1968. Group assigned him to Company C, in Da Nang, for duty with Team A-101 at Lang Vei. The team needed a combat engineer of his rank.

One of the U.S. Army's myriad forms is DA Form 2496-1. Its purpose is to comply with yet another army regulation concerning notification of next of kin if the soldier is "slightly wounded." Phillips chose not to have his mother notified if he suffered such a wound.

Specialist Fifth Class Phillips's service records also included two very important dates: his date of expected return from overseas service (DEROS) and his end-of-enlistment date. His DEROS was 10 January 1969; his enlistment would expire 17 March 1969.

Team sergeant Bill Craig took each replacement under his wing as soon as he arrived in country. The combat veteran enhanced those subjects that the new guy had first learned in Special Warfare School but needed to engrave into his subconscious if he was to survive. Since Specialist Fifth Class Phillips was the only recent replacement, he would be the lone recipient of the battlefield and bush knowledge of a real combat professional. He learned the "bunker theory" that Craig taught: the value of getting out of his bunker as soon as possible during an attack in order to be able to fire and maneuver.

Craig assigned Dan Phillips to join him on the western end of the perimeter, operating an 81mm mortar in the event of enemy attack. The veteran and the rookie shared a bunker next to their mortar pit.

The perimeter had the shape of a dog bone, or perhaps a roasted peanut in the shell. The long axis of the camp ran almost east-west. Within the perimeter, protected by triple concertina, double apron, and some German razor wire, were originally almost three hundred CIDG, mostly South Vietnamese, and a growing number of Bru tribesmen.

The next-higher headquarters for the Lang Vei Special Forces unit was Company C in Da Nang, which was nearly one hundred miles away. The Green Berets at Lang Vei were the basic unit of Special Forces: the A-Team. Originally an A-Team had consisted of one officer and eight enlisted men. That makeup changed to two officers and ten enlisted men. A B-Team, composed of a major commanding three officers and nine enlisted men, coordinated the A-Teams. The C-Team, commanded by a lieutenant colonel, with two officers and nine enlisted men, served as the command group to act as liaison with the senior indigenous personnel. The C-Team was also responsible for developing the strategy necessary to accomplish a given mission. The A-Team then would be the basis of Green Beret operations and could operate semi-independently in remote, unfriendly areas.

3
The MIKE Force

Lt. Col. Daniel F. Schungel commanded Company C of the 5th Special Forces Group (Airborne). Schungel was a man with a long and varied military background that began when he attended a military school as a high-school student. He graduated in June 1944, just in time to serve a two-year hitch in the U.S. Navy as an enlisted man. Like many others of his era, Schungel went to college after his discharge from the military. He attended the University of Kansas but completed his degree at Wichita State University, receiving his Reserve Officers Training Corps (ROTC) commission in 1950. Schungel immediately fell in love with the U.S. Army. Following a one-year competitive tour at Fort Riley, Kansas, he won a regular army commission in 1951, at the age of twenty-five. The regular commission was essential to a successful military career for an officer.

Luckily for the North Koreans and the Chinese communists, the young lieutenant headed east instead of west. Schungel served a three-year tour with the 12th Infantry Regiment of the 4th Infantry Division in Germany, beginning in 1951, when he landed with the advance party. He completed jump school in 1956, then went on to Korea for a sixteen-month tour, returning in early 1958. Two tours in the Kansas flatlands followed, first at Fort Riley, then Fort Leavenworth.

The next stop was the five-sided insane asylum called the Pentagon, where the biggest prize is a good parking spot, second only to finding the male officers' latrine on the first day of duty. In February 1963, it was again ticket-punching time on the way up the promotion ladder. Now it was Norfolk, Virginia, and the Armed Forces Staff College, from which Schungel graduated in July 1963.

In September 1963, he found himself in South Vietnam, serving as an adviser to the Army of the Republic of Vietnam. A year later it was a command billet, and he served as a battalion commander in the 10th Mountain Division in Fort Carson, Colorado. Next came an interesting tour in the basement of the Pentagon, with a varied civilian and military group that included an anthropologist and a psychologist. The study group had the abbreviation PROVN—the Program for the Pacification and Long Term Development of South Vietnam. Whether or not the nine-month tour ever really accomplished anything is unknown.

After a tour at the Army War College, the next logical step was a combat command. Lt. Col. Daniel F. Schungel arrived in Da Nang, South Vietnam, in June 1967, to take over Company C of the 5th Special Forces Group (Airborne), 1st Special Forces.

What kind of man was Dan Schungel? The comment of another Special Forces Officer, 1st Lt. Paul

Longgrear, says it all to those who have served their country: "Schungel was an E-7 in a lieutenant colonel's uniform." It was high praise coming from a man who would leave Vietnam on a stretcher, suffering from multiple combat wounds, with a chest full of ribbons as multicolored as a fruit salad. Schungel had a close-cropped iron-gray flattop, capping a fat-free body an inch or so short of six feet tall. He packed a rock-solid 175 to 180 pounds. The angry eagle with spears in its talons tattooed on his right forearm sent a signal from this rugged-looking character: if you mess with the bull, you get the horns. Schungel was the caricature of a tough combat leader, a man among men who stood out in a crowd. Known as a lean, mean fighting machine, he became an icon in Special Forces history. Schungel was the real thing in real time, the kind of guy you want on your side in a barroom brawl.

Serving under Schungel was veteran combat soldier and, like Bill Craig, one of the early members of Special Forces, Maj. Adam Husar, the commanding officer of the MIKE Force battalion. Husar had performed a number of behind-the-lines missions in the Korean War. He joined the 77th Special Forces Group (Airborne) in 1955, and in December 1960, by then a captain, he went into Vietnam from Okinawa on a covert mission as part of a four-man team along with Maj. Jack Warren and two senior enlisted men. Husar began this tour in III Corps, near the Saigon River. After less than a month, he saw that he could not work for his B-Team commanding officer and sought more congenial quarters in I Corps. Lt. Col. Dan Schungel, the Company C commander, said that Husar could be his Company C executive officer, or head the MIKE Force. Husar took the MIKE Force.

On 22 December 1967, Schungel had dispatched a MIKE Force company to Lang Vei to lend assistance to Captain Willoughby's A-Team. The MIKE Force consisted of six Green Berets and a company of Hre montagnards numbering just a few men shy of two hundred. First Lieutenant Longgrear, formerly a platoon commander, was on 22 December just completing his first week as company executive officer of the MIKE Force company.

Paul Richard Longgrear was born in Cairo, a sleepy town of just over ten thousand souls in southern Illinois, on 23 July 1943. His father, a traveling salesman, left town on a sales trip the day he was born and never returned. His mother took him to Jonesboro, Arkansas, where he grew up doing pretty much what he pleased. Tall, good-looking, popular with the girls, and deeply hurt by his nonexistent father, Longgrear acquired a reputation as a problem waiting for a place to happen. Worse, he felt it necessary to live up to the reputation even though he found that his actions and personality were not even acceptable to himself.

By the time Longgrear was a senior at Jonesboro High School, things looked good for him, at least on paper. Elected president of his graduating class, an important cog on the football team, Longgrear should have enjoyed a good senior year before going off to college or to a new life. But he told the football coach to take his sport and shove it, and then he got into trouble with the law. He found himself on the expulsion list with three days' unplanned vacation during which an important exam took place in his English class. He failed English and school officials prohibited him from conducting the first class assembly: Jonesboro did not need an example like Paul Longgrear as its standard bearer for the senior class. Before long Paul was on his way to Culver, Oregon, to try to finish high school.

But the new start became the old routine. Nevertheless, he managed to find enough spare time to squeak through with a high-school diploma.

College, with its need for self-discipline, did not do much for Paul Longgrear, and he left Arkansas State in December 1964. Longgrear went to California, up and down the coast on various construction jobs. His pursuit of a carefree, or perhaps aimless, lifestyle ended abruptly with a telegram: "Greetings, Mr. Paul R. Longgrear."

The U.S. Army drafted Paul R. Longgrear in June 1965. While for most people a draft notice ranks right up there in popularity with an eviction notice or a subpoena, for Longgrear it was a challenge. The eighteen-hour days in basic combat training at Fort Polk, Louisiana, definitely not a popular summer vacation spot, challenged a young man who had never succeeded at anything for long. But he had the raw materials for the job, and the army had the supervisors to see that the job was performed correctly. Longgrear had found a home.

Longgrear looked on the rigors of basic training as an obstacle to be overcome, and he persevered. He found pleasure in both the physical and mental demands. Graduation day at Fort Polk found Pvt. Paul R.

Longgrear the proud recipient of the outstanding trainee award.

His next obstacle was Advanced Individual Training (AIT) at Fort Ord, California. Longgrear finished second out of 220 soldiers in the skills of the infantryman, and he was rewarded by being selected to remain at Fort Ord as part of the permanent cadre. His immediate assignment was Drill Instructor School.

By this time the war in Vietnam had become a prime concern. The evening news carried the bloodshed into the living rooms of America, and Paul Longgrear saw Vietnam as his first choice for his next duty station. He needed to prove himself equal to the challenge of combat.

Unfortunately, the Department of the Army saw the situation a bit differently, and a disappointed young soldier found that the Drill Instructor School had a higher priority than the next quota of foot soldiers headed for Vietnam. Most rational men do not look forward to combat. Paul Longgrear, cut from a different cloth, wanted to go in harm's way. He saw Drill Instructor School as a roadblock that would take him at least a year to overcome, and he fired out request after request for transfer to Vietnam. Not many young soldiers just out of AIT would have the nerve to call the Pentagon directly to try to expedite a trip into war. None of his attempts succeeded in getting him on that plane to Southeast Asia, but it was obvious to his superiors that this was a young man with a purpose in life.

Longgrear soon found that there was only one priority higher than Drill Instructor School, and that was Officer Candidate School. Officer Candidate Paul R.

Longgrear saw his time at Fort Benning, Georgia, as an opportunity, an express ticket to combat in Southeast Asia. Secretly he hoped that the war would outlast his six months of officer training. On 26 May 1966, 2d Lt. Paul Richard Longgrear received his infantry commission in the U.S. Army. His first job would be to stay right at Fort Benning's OCS to teach infantry tactics to the candidates.

During a cycle break between OCS classes, Second Lieutenant Longgrear was eligible to use some well-earned leave. The July and August Georgia heat and humidity were nearly unbearable, and Longgrear decided that it would be a good time to cool off by jumping out of airplanes. He successfully applied for jump school.

Receiving his jump wings in the sweltering heat of August 1966, he was not to attend jump-master school until he had become an ROTC professor at Florida Southern College in the early seventies.

In the meantime, during his OCS days as a tactics instructor and during jump school, Longgrear had established himself in the many bars and hangouts of Columbus, Georgia. This time of rapid troop buildup, both stateside and in Vietnam, was a nonstop party near bases that saw troops moving in, training, and moving out to the war. Longgrear's schedule was a killer. It was army training from 0500 to 2100, then on to Sin Town until 0200. He did this six and sometimes seven days a week.

But all that changed for Paul Longgrear on 10 September 1966. It was a warm Sunday afternoon in Columbus, and he had stopped in a store for a few supplies. There he met Patty Jackson, a Georgia peach of the marrying kind. Engaged on 10 October 1966, the couple were married at the Fort Bragg chapel on 10 December 1966.

Pathfinder School was five weeks of arduous training: detailed map reading, demolitions, and drop-zone and landing-zone operations. Longgrear learned to parachute into hostile territory and set up either a drop zone for incoming paratroops or a landing zone for heli-borne air mobile troops. He also qualified to run mass paradrops or helicopter landing zones for air assault operations. Finally, he became adept at establishing and maintaining a fixed-wing, field expedient runway for loading or unloading and refueling aircraft.

Longgrear and a future comrade in arms, Frank C. Willoughby, went through the four-month weed-out process of the Special Forces officer qualification course and graduated together. They met the tactical, physical, and mental requirements that would stand them in good stead in mortal combat.

First Lieutenant Longgrear arrived in Da Nang on 12 November 1967. He soon found out that the A-Team rosters were full. The last thing he wanted was a staff job at this point in his career. Combat commands are the foundations on which to build successful military careers. He narrowly missed the assignment as intelligence officer of Company C, 5th Special Forces Group (Airborne). Fortunately another lieutenant arrived in the nick of time, and Longgrear went temporarily to the MIKE Force, moving on to Lang Vei and Team A-101. It was 15 November, and Longgrear went to observe the turnover of MIKE Force companies, as a fresh company replaced one that had been there for a designated time. Longgrear's assignment was to the company composed of Rhade montagnards.

His first night in the field on 17 November was at the OP that his MIKE Force would one day occupy. It was about seven hundred meters west of the New Lang Vei camp, and at that time it had no wire or defensive warning systems, because the unit was only temporarily at Lang Vei. The montagnards impressed Longgrear when he checked the guard posts at 0230 and found all the guards well concealed and wide awake.

The next day he got a call from his commanding officer, who told Longgrear to prepare to move his platoon out at 1730 for an ambush operation that would last about twelve hours. Longgrear returned the next morning disappointed because the ambush had turned out to be unproductive, but it had given him a chance to see his platoon operate under combat conditions.

Returning to Da Nang, Longgrear became executive officer of 12 Company, composed of Hre montagnards, on 16 December. The new company was not as good as the Rhade, but Longgrear determined that they would improve in a hurry. Several days later he received orders that the company would be in Lang Vei on 22 December, just in time to become settled in for Christmas. The intent was for the MIKE Force company to be in Lang Vei for at least thirty days. Longgrear wrote home to his father-in-law, Col. Fred O. Jackson, a retired army officer. His letter included a startling awareness of what the future held: "Intel says [the New Lang Vei Special Forces camp] is supposed to be overrun around Tet. It will be hairy if they do.

There is a regiment (4 battalions) [NVA] less than 3 ks away in Laos. . . . Look for Lang Vei (A-101) in the newspapers."

Out of Longgrear's 170-man company, which included five "round eyes" (U.S. Special Forces), only 75 had made it by 22 December. The next day the rest of the company still had not arrived, but that did not stop those at Lang Vei from improving their defensive positions. They went to work setting up antipersonnel Claymore mines and installing listening posts (LPs) beyond their perimeter to provide that all-important early warning of the approach of hostiles.

The closest the Lang Vei camp would come to the holiday spirit was an aircraft flying over it playing Christmas songs on a loudspeaker system. Santa Claus apparently stayed in the aircraft, but he did manage to drop some magazines for the troops. Longgrear thought of the marines only a few miles away involved in a holiday firefight, and then of the lucky pilot who would return to Da Nang for a Christmas celebration.

The young lieutenant had already seen some action and even picked up a crossbow on one operation. The Hill Fights for the marines near Khe Sanh signaled the start of something big.

On 23 January the MIKE Force outpost was "strafed by the Air Force, bombed by the Navy and had short artillery rounds put on us by the Marines," Longgrear wrote home. "This place is starting to get on my nerves." He became company commander a week later while hospitalized in Da Nang for dysentery. He had left the MIKE Force on 28 January; three days later he returned as its commander.

. . .

LONGGREAR'S GREEN Beret platoon leaders in the MIKE Force were Sfc. Charles Lindewald, a heavy-weapons specialist; Sfc. Harvey G. Brande, senior medic; Sfc. Earl Burke, a heavy-weapons specialist; and Sgt. John Early, a light-weapons specialist. Longgrear also commanded Sp4c. James L. Moreland, a medic.

While he had already seen combat as a platoon leader and company executive officer, this assignment would be the first combat command for Longgrear and, like Dan Phillips, he had his own mentor. Phillips had had Bill Craig, and Longgrear was fortunate to have a veteran warrior to teach him those tricks of the trade that tend to prolong life in combat. The young lieutenant came under the wing of Charlie Lindewald, a man who knew just about all there was to know about fighting in Southeast Asia. He had arrived in Vietnam with one of the first A-Teams, A-113, some six years before, and he had only left for extension leave and an occasional rest-and-recreation trip. He wore a tiger's tooth on a chain around his neck, from a tiger that he had killed. Lindewald told Longgrear, "A cat only has nine lives and I'm already past that. Percentages will catch up with me eventually."

Charlie Lindewald took a liking to the young lieutenant, who was eager and willing to learn from an old Indochina hand. He told Longgrear that if anything happened to him, Longgrear was to take the tooth and wear it. Longgrear soon found out that Lindewald was only comfortable in the bush, and that he was out of his element in a noncombat situation. Absolutely fearless in combat, the bearded "noncom" was the type of man you put up with between wars, so that he'd be there when you needed him—when the shooting started.

The MIKE Forces were distinct from the CIDG, which normally served in their own living area and had their own tribesmen as officers. Led by Green Berets, the MIKE Forces received more thorough training and became airborne qualified. They were mercenaries, to be sent wherever needed. In addition to their regular pay, they received bonuses according to the number of captured enemy weapons they returned after each battle. With four of his Green Berets as platoon commanders— Specialist Fourth Class Moreland was the medic and not in a command billet—Lieutenant Longgrear was intensely training his company of Hre. Under prior company and platoon commanders, they had acquired a reputation for breaking under fire. Longgrear had been executive officer for just a week before being sent to this northwest corner of Quang Tri province. During his brief time with the MIKE Force company, Longgrear had seen much improvement in the Hre troops.

Now, deep in Indian Country, the training intensified. As a result, the unit developed into a smoother-working combat machine. However, Captain Willoughby was careful, initially, to separate the mercenary Hre from his Bru CIDG. Longgrear to this day believes that at least part of the reason was that the Hre tried to purchase the Bru women. Captain Willoughby assigned the Hre to the OP about seven hundred meters from the main camp, on the south side of Route 9. When they had first arrived, they had also served at an LP or set up ambushes at Lang Troai, just south of the camp. Lieutenant

Longgrear's patience finally ran out with Willoughby. His MIKE Force did more its share of the patrolling, and his NCOs complained of being overextended, tired, and nearly exhausted. Longgrear's MIKE Force platoon commanders were also unhappy that Willoughby did not allow their Hre inside the camp. Not even the American Special Forces of the MIKE Force could go inside the inner perimeter. Finally it came to a showdown between the two commanders.

Willoughby, a tough leader, would still listen to reason. He assigned one of his A-Team members to accompany one of Longgrear's MIKE Force platoon commanders at the OP west of camp each night. The Lang Troai LP was operational during the hours of darkness until about the last week in January. While Willoughby's and Longgrear's recollections of the events regarding the MIKE Force differ, there is one common point. At the time of the Tet Offensive, only one platoon of the MIKE Force manned the OP. Commanded by (technically advised by) two Green Berets each night, the OP had one NCO from the MIKE Force and one from the A-Team. Because the CIDG were severely understrength, the Hre were able to man the vacant reinforced bunkers.

The OP would probably be the first to feel any attack from the NVA, if they came from the west. It was the job of the Hre montagnards to patrol their surrounding area constantly, looking for signs of enemy activity. Their Green Beret platoon commanders continuously trained them, keeping them on the alert. Tactically, Longgrear thought that they were ready.

The MIKE Force patrols would range right up to the

Sepone River on the Laotian border, which the Green Berets had orders not to cross unless they were in "hot pursuit" of the enemy. More than a few times, the Green Beret platoon commanders radioed messages to the command bunker that they were in hot pursuit of an enemy force fleeing across the Sepone. The radio operator in the command bunker would hear bursts of rifle fire intended to convince anyone in doubt of the need to cross the river into Laos. Of such stuff are elite troops made.

4

The Role of the Green Berets

Who were these elite troops, and what were they doing in a far-off land carrying out a very unconventional war?

In November 1960, the American people elected a youthful president, John F. Kennedy, to lead them in a most uncertain time. The Cold War was on. The Soviets were cultivating another youthful leader in Cuba named Fidel Castro. Retiring President Eisenhower informed his energetic successor that Laos and Vietnam would require immediate attention, perhaps even troops. Eisenhower promised his Democratic successor that if Kennedy felt the need to send troops to Vietnam, he would come to Washington from his retirement home and stand with him in support of such action. Kennedy told James B. Reston, a *New York Times* reporter, that Vietnam might be the avenue to making U.S. power credible. Kennedy obviously wanted to show his toughness to Khrushchev. The Soviet premier had attempted to take advantage of Kennedy's youth and inexperience at a summit meeting in Vienna early in his presidency.

Premier Khrushchev had undoubtedly known of then-Senator Kennedy's stated belief that an independent Vietnam was important to American foreign policy. Two weeks prior to Kennedy's inauguration, the Soviet leader bluntly stated that communism would be the ultimate world leader, largely through the efforts of what he termed wars of national liberation. These, he said, would occur throughout the Third World. Khrushchev specifically mentioned his intention to fully support the struggle of the National Liberation Front in Vietnam.

Kennedy breached the limit for the number of advisers to the South Vietnamese that had been set by the 1954 Geneva Accords. President Eisenhower had strictly adhered to the limit during his term of office. President Kennedy also authorized U.S. military advisers to play a combat role with their advisees. The U.S. death count rose accordingly. An important aspect of Kennedy's character with regard to the Special Forces was that he was a voracious speed-reader who had a genuine interest in espionage, clandestine activities, and guerrilla warfare. Kennedy not only devoured Ian Fleming's James Bond spy novels, but also read Mao Tse-tung and Che Guevara on guerrilla tactics. The Special Forces had a real friend in JFK.

Kennedy as a senator was well read on the subject of counterinsurgency: the theory that the way to defeat guerrillas was by fighting them with better-trained and better-equipped guerrillas. He read of this theory's successes in the Philippines and Malaya. Kennedy also brought to Washington Walt Whitman Rostow, an academic from the Massachusetts Institute of Technology.

Kennedy named Rostow deputy national security adviser concentrating on Southeast Asia. Rostow was a specialist in international development and economic history. As such, he believed that the countries of the Third World were indeed, as Khrushchev had threatened, obvious and vulnerable targets for national wars of liberation. Communist agents would prepare them for the three phases of warfare, beginning with guerrilla warfare.

Laos in 1961 was perhaps even more of a trouble spot than Vietnam, but it was also less accessible, and U.S. support for the government and army there had recently failed. The Pathet Lao, with heavy North Vietnamese support, combined with neutralists against the U.S.-backed anticommunist Col. Phoumi Nosavan. They seized the Plain of Jars, a strategic central Laotian area. Kennedy's assessment of the Laos situation led him to choose Vietnam as a likelier candidate for effective U.S. assistance. Laos was landlocked, ruling out aid from the U.S. Navy. Also, it bordered two communist countries that would be able to supply it with aid much faster and more effectively than the United States could. Additionally, the Laotians tended to be less-effective fighters for their own freedom than were the Vietnamese. Walt Rostow told JFK in March 1961 that Nosavan's forces were not combat effective, as witnessed by their recent halfhearted losses to the much more dedicated, communist-dominated, and North Vietnamese–directed Pathet Lao.

Great Britain and France, both Southeast Asia Treaty Organization allies, turned down Kennedy's request for armed intervention to save Laos from the communists. Kennedy then considered unilateral U.S. action, which Eisenhower had suggested as a last resort. Special Forces units had been performing missions in Laos since early 1959. Kennedy even authorized the sending of a small contingent of marines to Thailand as a jumping-off spot for future Laotian operations. Unfortunately that move coincided with the ill-fated Bay of Pigs invasion of Castro's Cuba. Cuba embarrassed the president by annihilating the CIA-sponsored invaders within three days of their landing on 17 April 1961.

Meanwhile, Walt Rostow's work in studying the ever-growing problem in Southeast Asia continued unabated. The forty-four-year-old Rostow was an unlikely military planner, but he gave his president some sage advice. He was appalled by the restrictions under which U.S. helicopters and Special Forces troops in Vietnam were trying to work. The men of 1st Special Forces Group (Airborne), whose headquarters was on Okinawa, had been in Vietnam since 1957 as advisers. Rostow told the president that it was somehow wrong to be developing these capabilities without applying them in a crucial active theater—they were not, after all, saving them for the Junior Prom. Special Forces had another backer.

Kennedy stewed long and hard over conflicting advice on the Laotian situation. Army chief of staff, Gen. George H. Decker, advised him that the United States could not win a conventional war in Asia and that if we went in, we must consider bombing Hanoi and even China. He even suggested the possibility of using nuclear weapons. Similar advice came from Adm. Arleigh

Burke, chief of naval operations. Kennedy had no need for the press to suggest that he was considering using nuclear weapons in Vietnam. He was trying to save a tiny country that most Americans had no knowledge of, and for which they had little concern.

The first four months of Kennedy's administration were a real trial. Fortunately for JFK, the North Vietnamese felt that if they persisted in Laos, the United States would intervene in force. They viewed that intervention as detrimental to their primary aim, which was the unification of Vietnam. They agreed to a ceasefire and another Geneva conference on Laos, which convened on 16 May 1961. Whether Kennedy really would have intervened in Laos had not the North Vietnamese taken the initiative to terminate the hostilities is unknown.

Faced with the possibility of declining popularity due to the Cuban fiasco and the Laotian near miss, Kennedy had to do something about restoring U.S. prestige. His closest friend, adviser, and younger brother, attorney general Robert F. Kennedy, had asked him during the heat of the Laotian crisis where he would prefer to stand and fight in Southeast Asia. His answer had been Vietnam, partly because of its coastal location. It had some semblance of government at the time, although that was fast eroding. Also it had a larger, better-trained, and equipped army than that of Laos. At the request of Ngo Dinh Diem, the United States had sent Special Forces into South Vietnam in May 1960 to train South Vietnamese rangers.

In May 1961 Kennedy sent his vice president, Lyndon Baines Johnson, to Vietnam to visit Ngo Dinh

Diem, on a fact-finding mission as well as a show of support for the Diem government. Johnson conferred with Diem, discussing the use of U.S. combat troops against the communists while they continued their role of training, equipping, and advising the Army of the Republic of Vietnam troops. Meanwhile, Kennedy was making some decisions in Washington. They were, in light of later events, seemingly modest moves. The president increased what was then called the Military Advisory Assistance Group by one hundred men. More importantly, Kennedy showed his confidence in Special Forces by dispatching four hundred Green Berets to South Vietnam.

In the autumn of 1961, President Kennedy made a special visit to the Special Forces Special Warfare Center at Fort Bragg. This visit was notable in two ways. First, he officially authorized the wearing of the green beret by the U.S. Special Forces. Second, he alerted the army high command (which had so often stifled the growth of Special Forces during the fifties) that he wanted immediate action taken to increase the capabilities of Special Forces. Army Special Forces soldiers, now known as Green Berets, knew that they had a friend in President John F. Kennedy. After his assassination, they renamed their training facility the John F. Kennedy Special Warfare Center.

The opposition of the traditional army leaders to the growth of Special Forces is significant. Obviously, they did not want their own roles diminished in any way. Their role was conventional warfare, and that is what they trained for and where they wanted to devote their resources. In addition, Green Berets trained for unconventional warfare. The training was not inexpensive and required the most modern weaponry and equipment. Outside the army, the various intelligence agencies—especially the CIA—were extremely conscious of any usurping of their territory by Special Forces.

The caliber of man required for service in Special Forces is high, as illustrated by the rejection rate for candidates for the Green Berets, which was 90 percent in 1962. Although the rejection rate dropped to 30 percent in 1964 as the size of the forces increased, it is important to note that not just any soldier could volunteer and automatically become a candidate. The preselection process weeded out those who were obviously unfit. A much-publicized attention-getter for the Green Berets was the public demonstration of their special skills. The most talked-about survival technique was that of catching, skinning, and eating a snake. In years to come the Green Berets would also carry the name "snake eaters."

Because of their training and administrative makeup, the Green Berets became the prime candidates for carrying out the counterinsurgency doctrine espoused by President Kennedy and directed by the CIA in South Vietnam. Some called it "winning the hearts and the minds of the people."

Others called it civic action, combined with self-defense. Sir Robert Thompson, head of the British Advisory Mission in Saigon, who had served previously as Britain's secretary of defense in Malaya, presented a formal paper to the U.S. government. In it he made suggestions intended to help win the war in Southeast Asia, as the British had won a similar war in Malaya. Thompson's analysis showed that the Viet Cong were intent on gaining control of the estimated sixteen thousand villages and hamlets in South Vietnam. Their method was persuasion backed by force. In other words, if political persuasion failed, cut off the village chief's head or disembowel his family in front of him, and you would have control of the village and its people and resources. This is how the Viet Cong gained supplies, intelligence, and recruits.

To counter this strategy, Thompson suggested the use of the "oil spot" theory. That theory would send an A-Team into a village, secure it, and gain the people's confidence by helping them medically and economically, as well as by supplying them with food. The A-Team would then help fortify the village, arm the people, and train them to use the weapons to defend themselves. If the internal defense proved inadequate, a relief force had to stand ready to assist. These actions would win the support of the people, and, denied their cooperation, the Viet Cong could not exist in that area. The A-Team would then move on to the next village and repeat the procedure. As these actions moved forward like the spreading of an oil spot on cloth, the Viet Cong would lose control of the entire area.

The British method, known as the "Strategic Hamlet Program," expedited the program by moving entire villages to a previously constructed fortified compound. With the additional protection, training time diminished significantly. Thompson argued that this practice would work even better in Vietnam than in Malaya.

The Viet Cong, forced to travel greater distances to obtain supplies and recruits, would hopefully venture into areas he called "killing zones." Caught in large numbers in exposed positions, the guerrillas stood greater risk of annihilation. He also foresaw the positive effect that the Saigon government could have on the villagers. By offering them safety from the Viet Cong, the government could also win them over with improvements to their standards of living. These improvements could take the form of new schools, wells, increased crop production, and medical-treatment facilities. His dream sounded good to Washington bureaucrats, who had no idea that most villagers would not leave their lifelong homes, humble as they were, for the protection of a corrupt government.

In an effort to reward cooperating villagers, Diem doled out government funds to those provinces whose reports of this type of pacification were superior. The system looked good on paper for a time. Money flowed into political subdivisions more rapidly and in greater amounts if their administrators' reports on pacification were positive—even if the actual situation was different.

The initial mission of the Green Berets occurred in 1957. Members of the newly formed 1st Special Forces Group (Airborne) arrived in Vietnam on temporary duty to assist in training South Vietnamese at the Nha Trang Commando Center. By 1962 ten A-Teams were deployed in the area of the village of Buon Enao in Darlac Province. The Rhade tribe lived there, and fifty tribesmen volunteered for the CIA's CIDG program on 15 December 1961. With the help of the

Green Berets, the Rhade volunteers soon became a relatively well-trained military force.

It must be understood that the Rhade tribesmen were montagnards (mountain people of Indonesian and Thai descent, as opposed to ethnic Vietnamese, the descendants of invading Mongols). The Rhade were quite different from their fellow Vietnamese who populated the cities and river deltas. The montagnards had darker skin and rounder faces and eyes, as distant relatives of the Indonesians. Uneducated and primitive, they lived at the bottom of the social scale in Southeast Asia, especially in Vietnam. Very rarely would they travel more than the distance they could cover in one day. They did not know who was in charge in Saigon, and they did not care. An atmosphere of distrust and animosity existed between the mountain people and the Saigon government. Saigon saw the U.S. advisers who were training the montagnards as encouraging montagnard independence, and its animosity increased. The ethnic Vietnamese called these montagnards *moi,* or savages.

President Diem and his increasingly powerful brother, Ngo Dinh Nhu, did not pay much more than lip service to the CIDG program, but they did like the strategic-hamlet idea. In early 1962 Nhu announced that the entire rural population would be included in the strategic-hamlet program. The Ngo brothers felt that it was politically in their best interests, as it would provide a place for the government to influence the population all the way to the tiniest hamlet, and, in effect, a way to control the voters and allow themselves to continue in power for as long as they desired. Conceptually

Nhu saw the idea as the way to get rid of the Viet Cong and the Americans at the same time.

While the Ngo brothers plotted a dynasty, the Green Berets continued their work. The CIA was especially happy with the progress on the CIDG program and asked for more Green Berets. However, this timing coincided with a buildup in American forces that resulted in the military's wanting to take control of the Special Forces from the CIA. The army, as discussed below, eventually won the fight to control its own Special Forces.

The role of the Green Berets in Vietnam, commanded by Col. George C. Morton beginning in September 1962, evolved into a mission designed to advise and assist the South Vietnamese government. The Green Berets would help to recruit, organize, train, equip, and then employ the CIDG forces. The CIA remained in charge of the CIDG program, and by the end of 1962 the Green Berets had 38,000 trained CIDG under arms. The training of the CIDG by the Green Berets became the responsibility of the U.S. Army under the U.S. Military Assistance Command, Vietnam during Operation Switchback, on 1 July 1963. On 26 October 1963, the Green Berets assumed responsibility for border surveillance.

The U.S. Special Forces continued to carry out their assigned mission of counterinsurgency. Beginning in 1963, their role changed from training the CIDG and various South Vietnamese elite units to more of an offensive role. By the close of 1967, there were A-Teams scattered throughout Indian Country, including a camp at Lang Vei, on Route 9 between the marine fire base at Khe Sanh and the Laotian border.

Every Special Forces soldier had a specialty. One might be a radio man, another an intelligence specialist, another a weapons specialist, and another a medic. But first, last, and always, the Green Beret was an elite fighting man.

5
The Pucker Factor Increases

One of the idioms widely used by American troops in the Second Indochina War was the Pucker Factor. In simplest terms, it means that as your situation becomes increasingly dangerous, the tighter the sphincter of your rear orifice becomes. Hence the correlation with danger is in direct proportion to your Pucker Factor.

Captain Willoughby and Sergeant First Class Craig had positioned their CIDG to effectively secure the perimeter. As close as the Green Berets were to the CIDG, the Americans always knew that the day might come when it was only them against the world, with no CIDG. Because of this, the Green Berets established an inner perimeter, of which the Tactical Operations Center, or command bunker, was the center. The Green Berets placed their bunkers along the edge of the inner perimeter and allowed only Americans inside this final protective barrier after nightfall. There were two exceptions: Vietnamese Special Forces (VNSF) Lieutenant Pham Duy Quan, who was the CIDG camp commander, and VNSF Sergeant Major Day, the operations chief. Even Frank and Jesse, Willoughby's bodyguards, stayed just outside the door to the TOC. Willoughby did not want the highly classified information inside the TOC in hands he could not trust, so he greatly limited the exposure. Willoughby often met with the camp commander, the operations officer (Lieutenant Quy), and the sergeant major in the team house to plan operations while keeping indigenous-personnel exposure to the TOC at a minimum.

Willoughby placed each of his four companies (one Bru and three Vietnamese) in the corners of the dog-bone ends. In the northwest sector was 102 Company; 103 was in the southwest sector; 104 (Vietnamese and his best company) in the southeast; and 101, the Bru, in the northeast, along Route 9 closest to Khe Sanh.

In the long midsection, Willoughby placed what he believed were his best Vietnamese and Bru troops. The 1st Combat Reconnaissance Platoon (CRP) manned the north-central perimeter paralleling Route 9. The 2d CRP had the south-central perimeter, while the 3d CRP was along the eastern wire, in the rear of 101 Company near the POL (petroleum, oils, and lubricants) dump. Two of the CRPs were Bru, whom Willoughby had begun training for expansion into a CRP Company. The other was Vietnamese.

Frank Willoughby, Bill Craig, and Paul Longgrear all insist, in contradiction to other reports, that the Lang Vei camp had only one 4.2-inch (four-deuce) mortar. The four-deuce mortar pit was on the crown of the hill near the TOC. Previous confusion may have been caused by the fact that the Green Berets built two 4.2-inch mortar pits, and Willoughby had an 81mm mortar in the second pit.

Some of the ammunition for the big mortars had manufacture dates of 1941 and 1942. A packing case held only two rounds of the aged ammo, taped together; fire ants and other insects had fed on the packing cases. The failure-to-fire rate as the A-Team practiced H and I (harassment and interdiction) and illumination fire was unacceptable. Willoughby remembers having to tip over the big mortar tube more than once to carefully slide out a round that had failed to fire. Many rounds that did fire traveled only a fraction of their intended flight of three kilometers. Willoughby also had seven 81mm mortars and nineteen 60mm mortars interspersed throughout the perimeter.

There were two key factors that would largely determine the ultimate fate of the camp. The first was the presence of only two of the American arsenal's deadliest weapons against tanks: the 106mm recoilless rifle. The A-Team's TOE (table of organization and equipment) did not provide a 106mm recoilless rifle. But Willoughby, not the average young captain, sent his ace scroungers—Craig, Hanna, and Charlie Lindewald (while assigned to A-101 prior to his tour with the MIKE Force)—to Da Nang. They brought back two 106s and as much ammunition as they could carry. The ammo consisted of about ten HEAT (high-explosive antitank) rounds and approximately six rounds of a new ammunition: flechette. This was a canister type, called "beehive rounds" by the Green Berets. These antipersonnel shells were similar to the double-canister grapeshot that had poured out of the business end of Civil War cannons over one hundred years earlier. It could tear huge holes in the ranks of oncoming infantry in close proximity. One beehive round covered an area two hundred meters in width, fired from a range of two hundred meters. Approximate coverage was one "killer bee" for every foot of frontage. They could tear an advancing line of skirmishers to ribbons. Only the Green Berets could operate the four-deuce mortar and the 106mm recoilless rifles.

Not only were there only two antitank rifles, there also was a severe shortage of HEAT rounds with which to arm them. Although it has previously been reported that there were forty rounds of the tank-killing ammunition, Longgrear remembers hearing that there were as few as ten.

Another major factor in determining the fate of the camp was the lack of antitank mines in the outer-perimeter wire. Barbed wire, used for many years as a defensive barrier, channelizes the attacking infantry into interlocking fields of fire covered by heavy automatic weapons, such as machine guns. The tanks that often accompany an infantry attack can roll right over the wire, but there was no record of any enemy tanks used in the attack in the nearly three years of heavy American involvement. While there is disagreement among those interviewed, both Willoughby and Craig say they had standing orders not to use antitank mines anywhere that they had indigenous personnel inside the perimeter. The defenders of Lang Vei set the Claymores, the deadly directional antipersonnel mines, for command detonation.

When the Green Berets heard of the plight of the 33d Laotian Battalion (overrun by tanks and infantry on 24 January), they requested and received airdrop shipments of light antitank weapons. Additionally, helicopters delivered more light antitank weapons (LAWs). Captain Willoughby remembers returning from R and R in Hawaii, flying in from Da Nang on 29 January with Lieutenant Colonel Schungel. The two shared space in their chopper with a small shipment of LAWs. Team A-101 had one hundred of these one-shot throwaway weapons, with each man in the team trained in their use and over half having recently fired them. At least ten CIDG had also fired the LAWs for familiarization (fam-fired). The LAWs, designed as tank killers, also worked well against bunkers and other hard targets. When Willoughby had left on R and R, he had had no positive knowledge of any tank threat against his camp. When Schungel radioed Willoughby that he would be sending him some M72 LAWs, the infantry captain told his commanding officer that they would make excellent weapons against snipers tied into trees.

The camp had only two of the relatively new M-60 7.62mm machine guns, but they also had two of the aged but powerful .50-caliber machine guns and thirty-nine of the World War II BARs (Browning automatic rifles). Most of the CIDG carried M-1 and M-2 carbines, of World War II and Korean War vintage. The CIDG did not even have the more modern M-14 7.62mm rifles, or the new M-16 5.56mm rifles that had caused the marines in the Hill Fights so much trouble.

Captain Willoughby actually had more weapons than he really needed, as long as they functioned as intended. Willoughby also knew that he had, as of 14 January, two rifle companies of marines ready to move on foot or by helicopter to his rescue, should the need arise. The marines could not just race their M-35 trucks down Route 9, as the NVA would surely have an ambush waiting for them. Willoughby also knew that a helicopter landing on a hot LZ could prove a disaster to his relief force. Additionally, there were several MIKE Force companies standing by in Da Nang. The captain knew his situation was precarious, but that was part of life for the Green Berets. The tension increased for Captain Willoughby and his A-Team as headquarters received new intelligence reports. They knew the communists had captured Khe Sanh village on 21 January. Since Khe Sanh village lay between the Lang Vei camp and the marine combat base at Khe Sanh, only a helicopter rescue mission was feasible.

One of Longgrear's MIKE Force patrols crossed into Laos in hot pursuit of a fleeing enemy. The patrol discovered the telltale tracks of armored vehicles. The tracks were recent enough to indicate that the NVA, contrary to the belief of the senior marine commanders in I Corps, did in fact have tanks in the vicinity.

On 22 January the Khe Sanh combat base monitored a desperate cry for help on a tactical radio frequency. The caller was from a Laotian army post in Tchepone, just inside the Laotian border, about ten miles from Lang Vei. Three battalions of NVA infantry, spearheaded by at least seven tanks, were overrunning some forward elements of Laotian Battalion BV-33, commanded by Lieutenant Colonel Soulang. Two U.S. B-57 Canberra fighter-bombers and a FAC (forward air controller) aircraft flew to their rescue. The heavy mists were impenetrable even to the air-dropped million-candlepower flares. The aircraft returned without firing a shot or spotting a tank. The frantic radio calls from the besieged Laotian ended abruptly.

The twenty-fourth of January broke out cold and overcast as Maj. Adam Husar and Lt. Paul Longgrear flew west following Route 9 from Lang Vei toward the Laotian border in Husar's C and C (command and control) chopper. Husar commanded the MIKE Forces based in Da Nang, and as battalion commander of the mercenaries, he was Lieutenant Longgrear's immediate superior. Longgrear briefed Husar, who had only taken command of the MIKE Force about three weeks earlier, on the activities of his MIKE Force company in their TAOR. Much to their surprise, the two officers observed a long stream of indigenous personnel heading toward Lang Vei. They overflew the entire column, which stretched almost to the Laotian border.

Returning to Lang Vei, Husar walked down to Route 9 by himself. The MIKE Force battalion commander carried only his .45-caliber pistol, which he stuck under his belt in the middle of his back, under his jacket. He had already removed his web belt. Husar walked slowly through the head of the column, speaking Lao to the refugees, asking the Laotians where they were coming from and what was happening. They seemed frightened, not saying much and shoving and pushing each other. Husar went down the road, probably threading his way through over a hundred, perhaps two hundred, of them. Then he came to a break in the long line. As he contemplated his next move, he heard shots fired. Being alone, with no cover and no other Americans in sight, he did the only smart thing to do. He doubletimed back to the camp, where his helicopter was waiting.

Husar left immediately for Da Nang and went directly to Lieutenant Colonel Schungel to report what he had observed. He told Schungel it was happening on Route 9 in very close proximity to the Lang Vei Special Forces camp. He also related to the company commander how the local Bru were flocking in from the opposite direction, coming west from near Khe Sanh. Husar, a Korean War veteran, remembered well how the North Koreans had used hordes of refugees as a way of infiltrating United Nations positions, then attacking without warning.

"We're getting set up for a hit," Major Husar remembers telling Schungel. "I know their tactics. This is the same thing they did in Korea." Next he went to the U.S. Agency for International Development, a part of the U.S. Department of State that was charged with looking out for the indigenous civilians. "You've got to do something about all those refugees, they are going to get killed!" demanded Husar. Ignored by the U.S. government employees, Husar angrily returned to Lieutenant Colonel Schungel.

"We've got to have a field grade officer up there," replied Schungel. Husar did not understand why until recently, when he learned of how the Laotian colonel refused to talk to any American officer below the rank of major (field grade). Schungel immediately sent his executive officer, Maj. Wilbur Hoadley, to handle Lieutenant Colonel Soulang of the Laotian battalion. The three field grade U.S. Special Forces officers would rotate after about three or four days. The first day that Major Husar was to replace Lieutenant Colonel

Schungel, who had taken turns at Lang Vei with Major Hoadley, would be 7 February.

LONGGREAR GRABBED his two Hre bodyguards from the OP and waited in the middle of Route 9. He was in position before the unidentified group of indigenous personnel arrived. He does not remember seeing Major Husar on the road. Beyond the OP, the junglelike vegetation had overgrown Route 9. There was only a single trail that the Bru had chopped through the undergrowth. The first members of the long group of stragglers that appeared out of the trail were civilians. Longgrear motioned them to get off the one-lane road. The tall lieutenant stood alone in the middle of Route 9, with only his two bodyguards in the bushes just off the road on either side of him. The Laotians all seemed to be civilians, carrying cooking pots and babies, lots of babies. More than two thousand of the civilian refugees passed Longgrear in the next four hours before he finally saw the van of the Laotian troops.

It was a lengthy column of haggard-looking native troops that Longgrear watched closely for some time as they approached him. As they got closer, the young lieutenant could tell at a glance that these Orientals marching down Route 9 were no threat in their current condition. Longgrear recalled seeing the soldiers in the column discarding equipment as he and Husar flew west above them. It turned out that they were the 33d Royal Laotian Elephant Battalion (BV-33), preceded by their wives, children, and relatives, and also by water buffalo, other animals, and chickens. They had fled from their homeland after a battalion of NVA regulars using tanks had mauled some of their forward elements two days earlier, less than ten miles away at Tchepone, near Ban Houei Sane. The Laotians had called for American air support, which had arrived in time to knock out one tank. Although cut off from their base by the advancing NVA, the Laotians had escaped to South Vietnam.

U.S. aircraft escorted the Laotian battalion as it headed east on Route 9, toward the safety of the Khe Sanh combat base. The war-birds aided the escape by destroying a bridge just after the Laotians had crossed it. The NVA made no further attempts at attacking the Elephant Battalion, which had been friendly with Green Berets since 1965, when Khe Sanh had been a Green Beret outpost. There had been flights between Khe Sanh and Ban Houei Sane for supply runs in 1965, and since then for intelligence gathering and information exchange for U.S. forward air controllers and airborne command centers.

On 24 January, Longgrear awaited Major Husar's orders regarding the disposition of a body of troops this size. (Longgrear's instinct was to turn the column around and send it back where it came from, but that was a decision that he could not make when his commander was in the immediate area.) Unknown to Longgrear, the A-Team had received notice at 0800 that morning that the Laotians were en route toward them.

Maj. George Quamo, MACV-SOG's special projects officer, also heard the radio message. He flew his C and C chopper to Lang Vei to pick up Sfc. Bill Craig and fly over the stream of refugees that flowed down Route 9 from Laos. Craig's A-Team commander, Captain Willoughby, had departed on 19 January for R and R in Hawaii to get some much-needed stress relief, and he would not return until 29 January. There had been agreements at the highest levels that the Christmas and Tet holidays would bring a cease-fire and a lull in the fighting. Willoughby had not wanted to go, but Lieutenant Colonel Schungel had prevailed, sending off A-101's leader during a quiet time.

Longgrear's MIKE Force troops were almost all on patrols at this time, and it was only he and Sfc. Charlie Lindewald at the OP. When the Laotian soldiers finally reached Longgrear, he pointed his rifle at them and motioned to them to get off the road and drop their weapons in a pile. Longgrear maintains that the decision to disarm them was a "knee-jerk reaction." Finally an English-speaking Laotian lieutenant came up to Longgrear, probably concerned that the single Green Beret lieutenant was disarming the ragtag battalion. Longgrear put it to the Laotian lieutenant in the simplest terms possible, "If they are Oriental and carrying a weapon, it goes on the ground in the pile."

The 33d Royal Laotian Elephant Battalion numbered more than 500 soldiers. It also included 2,200 dependents, families, and camp followers, and a number of water buffalo. Major Quamo, flying over the Laotians with Sergeant First Class Craig, reported up to 6,000 Vietnamese and Laotian refugees and soldiers headed in the direction of Lang Vei. He estimated their time of arrival as approximately nightfall on 25 January. Due to the overgrown condition of Route 9 from

Longgrear's OP to the Laotian border, rapid movement for a group that size was impossible.

When Major Quamo contacted Company C headquarters in Da Nang regarding the arrival of the Elephant Battalion, he cited an immediate need for a field grade officer (major, lieutenant colonel, or colonel) and six additional Green Berets. Six Green Beret enlisted men arrived the next day, along with ammunition, food, and medicine. They also brought materials to help restore the destroyed defensive positions at Old Lang Vei. The executive officer of Company C in Da Nang, Major Hoadley, arrived to act as a liaison officer with the Laotians.

At 0830 on the morning of 26 January, Lieutenant Colonel Schungel, the commanding officer of Company C, and his civil-affairs officer, 1st Lt. Warren R. Orr, Jr., took off from Da Nang. En route, they stopped at Quang Tri to speak with province officials about the evolving situation. Lieutenant Orr spoke with the Civil Operations and Revolutionary Development Support (CORDS) senior adviser, Mr. Brewer. He asked what plans the province team had for assisting the thousands of expected refugees, with the problems that they would invariably bring with them and develop during their stay in the Lang Vei area.

Mr. Brewer was blunt. There was no help available. He told Lieutenant Orr that the decision from a level higher was that no evacuation would take place, and no food would be provided. It seemed time for the miracle of the loaves of bread and the fish. In addition, psychological warfare operations would provide a helicopter-mounted loudspeaker in the area that would advise the montagnard refugees who followed the Laotians to return to their homes and not come near any military encampments.

Lieutenant Orr next visited the civil-affairs company in the MACV compound. He asked what that group could do to help the refugees. He received the same answer that Mr. Brewer had given. There was apparently no intent of giving the Green Berets at Lang Vei any help from Quang Tri, the provincial capital, so Schungel and Orr continued on to Lang Vei, arriving at 1100. Lieutenant Orr made a survey of the area. He passed his findings regarding the situation and the projected needs on to Company C. There, civil-affairs officer 1st Lt. Walter R. Beardslee would work with the supply officer and CORDS in Da Nang to initiate the flow of supplies.

Within two hours, supplies headed toward Lang Vei in the form of a substantial airdrop. The Laotian battalion was at the Old Lang Vei camp, and the civilian refugees were populating the village of Lang Vei and its immediate vicinity. By 1700 the next day, rice, packages of indigenous rations, salt, milk, large canvas tarpaulins, and a paper blanket for each of the Laotians had been air-dropped on the supply drop zone at Lang Vei. These supplies would suffice until 10 February. Company C was going through channels to obtain government action in response to the refugee situation. The situation called for movement of the refugees, or for protection of them.

FIRST LT. MILES Wilkins, when he saw the long line of Laotian soldiers and refugees, thought of only one thing: "a big international incident." In front of him he saw more than two thousand people forced across their country's boundary into South Vietnam. What kind of international-relations problems would this incident cause? Wilkins, as executive officer, was in command until his commanding officer returned from R and R. He directed the supply aircraft that suddenly appeared over the large open area on the north side of the camp. They stacked up, coming in with low-level drops, mostly of canned food on pallets. Although the Laotians made little effort to even collect the food, there was one major—and tragic—exception.

A Laotian male dashed out onto the drop zone, and before anyone could react and remove him, a pallet loaded with canned food smashed into his face. There was an ugly sound as the fast-moving, solid object hit the small man, tearing his flesh and crushing his bones. Sgt. Nickolas Fragos, a medic, dashed to his aid. The Laotian was literally drowning in his own blood. Fragos attempted mouth-to-mouth resuscitation, but it proved unsuccessful. Next Fragos tried a tracheotomy tube, but that was too large for the small, dying patient. Finally Fragos whipped a ballpoint pen from his pocket, broke it, and plunged it into the man's throat as a field expedient tracheotomy. The scene is still vivid in Wilkins's memory. The Laotian was still alive when placed on a medevac chopper, but Wilkins never heard a further report.

The Laotians did not attempt to set up the tents that were airdropped to them, says Wilkins, and they did little to improve the destroyed defenses of the Old Lang Vei camp.

When he returned from R and R, Captain Willoughby accompanied Lieutenant Colonel Schungel to the Old Lang Vei camp to call upon the Laotian commanding officer, Lieutenant Colonel Soulang. While Lieutenant Colonel Schungel was looking at the defenses that the Laotians were supposed to be rebuilding, he found a lot of people leaning on shovels; there was not much movement. Willoughby got as far as the English-speaking lieutenant who had earlier spoken to Longgrear as the Elephant Battalion arrived.

Willoughby had come with interpreters prepared to speak with the colonel (one, a Rhade montagnard, spoke French, English, Vietnamese, and Bru; the other spoke Laotian). He had been unaware that the colonel spoke English, but the Laotian commander was not going to speak to a company grade (lieutenant or captain) officer anyway.

Schungel had already spoken with the colonel on his first trip, on 26 January, and had been told at that time that tanks leading units of the NVA 304th and 325th Divisions had attacked the Laotian battalion. The report did not satisfy Willoughby. He agreed with First Lieutenant Longgrear's on-the-spot estimate of the situation when he had intercepted the column upon its arrival. The Laotians were carrying no casualties, and their weapons looked too good to have come through such an ordeal so recently, with obviously little chance to do anything but flee. Willoughby returned some of the Laotian weapons. Team sergeant Craig gave the Laotians some old 3.5-inch rocket launchers, but would later come to regret it.

The U.S. Department of State, through its ambassa-

dor to Laos, William H. Sullivan, agreed that the move
to Old Lang Vei was the least undesirable of several
options, including moving them to Khe Sanh or evacu-
ating them by air back to Laos.

ON 30 January an NVA private, Luong Dinh Du, of 8th
Battalion, 66th Regiment, 304th Division, suddenly
appeared at the doorway of the team house, much to
the shock of the Green Berets. The wily veteran Craig
did not stop to consider how the NVA private had got
past the sleeping guards at the camp gate; instead he
grabbed the closest weapon, a whiskey bottle. Private
Du, carrying an AK-47 assault rifle, immediately threw
up his hands in surrender. Craig quickly realized that
this was a most unorthodox method of surrender, and
certainly not sufficient reason to break a perfectly
good bottle of whiskey over the man's head.

Private Du was a veteran of the NVA 304th Division.
On 20 January, a pitifully small number of U.S. Marines
and U.S. Army advisers had battered his infantry regiment in Khe Sanh village, with the help of air support.
Constant earth-shaking bombing attacks by B-52s that
he could not see had made the young private want to be
on the other team. From his unit's location, he could see
the Lang Vei Special Forces camp, and so he had just
slipped away during the night. He had been surprised to
walk unchallenged through the main gate of the camp.

Asked (with the help of crude drawings) whether he
had seen any tanks, the private replied that he had no
knowledge of them. The gift of such information is, of
course, subject to immediate skepticism. The private

told the Green Berets of an impending attack on their camp. In fact, he said, the camp had been the object of close reconnaissance by the battalion executive officer accompanied by a sapper squad (commandos specially trained in the use of demolitions) just two days before. The recon party had been there to determine the locations of the various weapons and to study the defensive setup of the camp. The NVA had postponed several planned attacks for various reasons, but it was just a matter of time before the attack commenced.

The Green Berets passed the private on to the marines at Khe Sanh. There, more intense interrogation determined that he had heard the noises made only by clanking tank treads but had never actually seen the tanks. The marines remained skeptical.

Also on 30 January, two other significant events occurred at the Lang Vei camp. Green Berets on patrol along the banks of the shallow Sepone River found an underwater road covered by just enough water to make it unobservable from the air. Captain Willoughby concluded that if the tanks did exist, the NVA would only use them as mobile fire support in the attack. He did not believe that they would use them to penetrate the perimeter. They would not waste precious armor on his small camp, but save it for the big push against the marine combat base at Khe Sanh. Nevertheless, it was at this point that the one hundred LAWs were air-dropped into Lang Vei camp.

The other significant event was the capture of one of the Green Berets who had been sent to Old Lang Vei on 25 January. Bill Craig had not been happy when Company C had told him they were sending him a specialist fourth class weapons expert. The man had been in country only a month. Previously assigned to the Special Forces B-Team at Da Nang, he had been responsible for Nung security forces guarding the B-Team compound. Craig had told the sergeant major that he would do without rather than have an inexperienced weapons man. But it was too late: Young was already on the way. Instead of keeping him at Lang Vei, Craig sent Sp4c. John A. Young to Sfc. Eugene Ashley, the senior man at Old Lang Vei, to help with the Laotians.

Frank Willoughby insists that, contrary to what has previously been reported, he did not send Young on a patrol with the Laotians. Bill Craig corroborates Willoughby's account, giving the following explanation of events: Craig received a call from Ashley one afternoon, saying that Young wanted to go on patrol. Craig told Ashley that Young was to stay in sight of the camp, and that the LP was as far as he could go. But Young talked the Laotians into going into Khe Sanh village, which was already in enemy hands. They found the enemy, but Specialist Fourth Class Young found to his great misfortune that the Laotians he was with had no stomach for battle. They fled, leaving him to try to fend off the NVA alone. The NVA captured Young and removed him from the scene of the brief one-sided battle.

Captain Willoughby's men, sensing impending trouble, improved the already formidable defenses of the Lang Vei camp. The Green Berets placed even more Claymore mines between the triple concertina entanglements. The mines' curved business ends would spew some seven hundred steel pellets when they were command-detonated by a pound and a half of C-4 plastic explosive. They were a nasty weapon indeed, and they had caused enough deaths to their installers that the words Front Toward Enemy soon appeared on the business side.

On 31 January, one of the MIKE Force patrols from Lang Vei was probing the area in the direction of Khe Sanh village, trying to get an estimate of the situation they were facing. As usual, there was much ground mist. There was, however, the unmistakable, pungent smell of *nuoc mam*, a fermented fish oil used as flavoring. It was obvious that the NVA were unaware of any visitors.

Suddenly the MIKE Force patrol found an opening in the blanket of fog and opened fire on a surprised NVA battalion. Following a short but lively firefight that included air strikes, the MIKE Force pulled back with a victory that claimed fifty-four NVA killed and thirty weapons for the bank accounts of the Hre mercenaries. Paul Longgrear relates the story of one of his Hre struggling with an NVA soldier, trying to wrestle his AK-47 away from him, perhaps thinking of his growing cash account. The Hre, suddenly no doubt remembering an easier way, blasted the NVA with his own weapon, facilitating the capture of the AK-47. A number of the NVA never made it out of their hammocks. Longgrear's Hre were learning their trade very well.

When Captain Willoughby got the news of this action, he decided that one MIKE Force platoon would suffice at the OP. The other platoons would help to strengthen the camp's defenses. Brande's MIKE Force platoon reinforced CIDG Company 101; Early's was sent to 104 Company; Lindewald's to 102 Company; and Burke's to the 1st Combat Reconnaissance Platoon.

Each night as one of the MIKE Force platoons went to the OP, the A-Team would adjust the perimeter to compensate for the absent manpower. The camp radio broadcast the news of the countrywide Tet Offensive. Willoughby knew he was in for big trouble.

The first five days of February passed with the Lang Vei defenders continuing their patrolling and watching and waiting, the worst part of being a soldier in the defensive posture. This was not the role the Green Berets had trained for, just as it was not the role the marines at the combat base at Khe Sanh had trained for. These were not boring days, however, because the NVA were registering their mortars and artillery, seemingly at the times that supply helicopters were landing or taking off from the Special Forces camp. One of those helicopters brought a visitor to Lang Vei. On the afternoon of 5 February, 1st Lt. Thomas E. Todd arrived at the camp. He was an engineer officer, sent to examine the airstrip for the purpose of repairing it.

On 6 February, the commanding officer of Company C, Lt. Col. Daniel Schungel, helicoptered in to relieve his exec, Maj. Wilbur Hoadley. Schungel would in turn be relieved the next day by the other field grade officer in the I Corps sector for Special Forces, Maj. Adam Husar, MIKE Force battalion commander. Wilbur Hoadley (incorrectly called Lieutenant Colonel Hoadley in a number of previous accounts) was a major at the time of the battle of Lang Vei, according to then-Capt. Max Cottrell, Company C's assistant operations officer in Da Nang.

The same day, Lieutenant Bailey, the team civil-affairs officer, flew to Da Nang for several days to take care of some personal matters. His job was to operate one of the 106mm recoilless rifles in the event of attack. Although Lieutenants Longgrear and Wilkins both now believe that no one operated Bailey's 106mm recoilless rifle during the battle, Captain Willoughby disagrees. He says he saw the weapon in operation as he dashed up the stairs of the TOC to assess the battle. Willoughby also states that each of the weapons operated only by the U.S. Special Forces had a primary operator and a backup.

The morning of 6 February brought mortar rounds screaming into the Lang Vei camp. The defenders returned fire with their 4.2-inch mortar. In the early evening, the defenders received another dose of the same medicine from Co Roc Mountain. Casualties were light, but nerves were getting a little frayed. Again the camp responded to the incoming with some outgoing of its own.

Lieutenant Longgrear performed his nightly ritual of sending a Hre platoon to the OP, this time under the command of Sergeant First Class Lindewald, accompanied by Sfc. Kenneth Hanna of the A-Team. Longgrear knew that they could not have gone much farther than the main gate when he heard a volley of rifle fire. The Hre mercenaries were rapidly returning to the safety of the camp. The two Green Berets, following their spooked platoon, reported immediately to Lieutenant Longgrear. Lieutenant Colonel Schungel joined them, trying to find out what had happened. The sergeants explained that the Hres had seen something—they believed it was many, many ("beaucoup!") VC—and panicked.

Longgrear again ordered the Hre to the OP, but they defiantly refused to go. Schungel was fuming. Longgrear explained to them the situation they were putting him in: making him and the sergeants look very bad in front of his commanding officer. He was appealing to the Oriental mind's concern about losing face, which they understood. He finally persuaded them to go.

At approximately 1800, the ground of the Lang Vei camp shook from an intense barrage of about fifty rounds of 152mm artillery fire from the direction of Co Roc Mountain. Counter-battery fire erupted from the marine artillery at the Khe Sanh combat base as well as from the camp's own 4.2-inch mortar. But the entire barrage from the marine guns landed in the wire on the camp's southern perimeter, in 104 Company's area, wounding two of the CIDG.

When the barrage ended, it was time for final preparations and last-minute checks. Lieutenant Colonel Schungel satisfied himself that the MIKE Force platoon now manned the OP. He took the Vietnamese Special Forces commander, First Lieutenant Quan, and the operations officer, First Lieutenant Quy, and checked the perimeter in the dying moments of daylight. The relationship between First Lieutenant Quan, who as camp commander was technically in charge, and Captain Willoughby, who was technically the senior American adviser, had not always been the best.

Just before occupying the new camp, the A-Team and their indigenous troops had stayed temporarily at the old camp. Captain Willoughby began to hear complaints that Lieutenant Quan would not lead operations outside the wire. Like many Vietnamese officers, he was a political appointee. At this time in his career, the hard-charging, gung-ho, no-nonsense Capt. Frank Willoughby was not very tolerant of fellow officers who would not lead from the front.

A showdown between the two, culminating in Willoughby's forcing Quan to perform a quick retreat toward Khe Sanh village, brought in two choppers carrying two brigadier generals, one Vietnamese and one American, plus other dignitaries including a high-ranking Special Forces officer from 5th Group headquarters, as well as Lieutenant Colonel Schungel. Willoughby was in serious trouble.

The captain received explicit orders to allow Lieutenant Quan back in camp. It was not a one-way conversation, however. The brass heard what Willoughby had to say. The upshot was that Quan would go on future operations, but one of the two of them would always be in the camp. After a forty-five-minute stay, the brass departed. They had not come for a tour of the camp; their sole purpose had been to let Quan return.

As WAS often the custom during the Second Indochina War, the troops turned in early if they were not on watch. They had a more than a fair chance of being rudely awakened during the early morning hours when "Charley" (the VC) came to call. Dan Phillips was one of those who hit the sack early. Paul Longgrear was sharing his bunker with Sgt. John Early, whose own bunker was still under construction. Bill Craig was still on duty.

At the Old Lang Vei camp, Sfc. Eugene Ashley was

the senior medic of the three-man team remaining of the six originally sent to inoculate the Laotian Elephant Battalion and their families against cholera. He was enjoying a beer and some conversation with his twenty-two-year-old associate, Sgt. Richard Allen. Ashley was proudly telling his unmarried friend about his wife and son back in the "real world."

6

Tank Attack

In combat, there are a number of triggers that can set off your reactions. Depending upon your situation at the time, the triggers can be much more subtle than a volley of rifle fire or the shock effect of a close round of incoming mortar or artillery fire. In Captain Willoughby's case, the past few days had been nerve-racking at best. It is always difficult to sit and wait for the enemy.

At about 1930, Captain Willoughby was in the command bunker. He received a radio call that the CIDG from 104 Company had heard noises that they thought were engines running. Soon thereafter, Sergeants Hanna and Lindewald called to report noises near the OP.

The OP next reported three trip flares being set off in their area at about 2100. They responded with illumination but were not able to see anything moving. A few itchy trigger fingers among the Hres at the OP fired in anticipation. As often happens, the bushes looked as if they were moving, and the NVA, masters of camouflage, might just have been those bushes. More of the OP defenders opened up, and soon the fever spread to the whole camp.

An hour later, 104 Company sprang into action when a trip flare went off in front of their lines. This time they were the ones to activate the nervous reaction of the rest of camp. The 50 percent alert went to 100 percent without an order having been given. Small-arms and automatic-weapons fire pierced the darkness, probing for victims but finding none.

During the daylight hours the weather had been clear, with the sky dotted by clouds at about two thousand feet. The quiet sky had come alive in the late afternoon, as the communist 152mm guns at Co Roc sent a message to the Green Berets at Lang Vei. It had been a calling card from the Laotian mountain.

As nightfall blanketed the camp, the tension level of those soldiers on guard increased markedly. Company C headquarters in Da Nang and the Special Forces camp at Pleiku, in II Corps, monitored the situation at Lang Vei by radio. Captain Willoughby did not answer all of the calls directed to him. Until the enemy action got close enough to force him inside the TOC, Willoughby ran up the stairs and climbed on top of the TOC, directing fire and air strikes. Radiomen Emanuel Phillips and Franklin Dooms handled the calls that were not urgent enough to call the A-Team commander from his observation of the developing battle. All of the following radio calls (noted by the time at which they were made) were monitored by Company C in Da Nang.

2230. Outposts report to Captain Willoughby (whose radio call sign was Spunky Hansen Six), underground in TOC, sporadic incoming mortar and artillery fire.

2240. Unknown station reports to Captain Willoughby a trip flare set off and most of the perimeter firing. Several stations demand of Willoughby, "Stop those Viets from firing!"

2310. Communications check with several stations from Captain Willoughby: no activity.

On top of the command bunker, or TOC, was a small observation tower. Sgt. Nickolas Fragos went on guard duty at 2200 on 6 February, for a three-hour shift in the tower. Fragos scanned the perimeter of the camp from its premier observation point. Just before midnight he had a visit from the team sergeant. Craig then returned to his bunker to try to grab some sleep while he could. Fragos had seen the reaction of the guard contingent to the trip flare in front of 104 Company. He also had seen how the friendly small-arms and automatic weapons had reacted to the illumination stimulus for about fifteen minutes before quieting down once again, waiting.

0030. MIKE Force OP (Sergeants First Class Lindewald and Hanna) to Captain Willoughby: "I think I have VC below me."

Fragos saw nothing remarkable again until about thirty minutes past midnight. Then he observed another trip flare go off in front of 104 Company on the southern perimeter, covering the trail to Lang Troai. It was in close proximity to the previous flare. This time he saw people. Two men were cutting the wire in front of two vehicles, which he could not immediately identify but soon realized were tanks. Fragos shouted into his radio handset to warn his commanding officer in the TOC below him. It was a classic understatement in a time of extreme crisis:

0035. Fragos in TOC tower to Captain Willoughby : "They've got tanks!"

Again 104 Company responded to the trip flare with a volley of fire. This time it terminated the wire cutters. One tank commander then turned on his tank's white searchlight and scanned the immediate area in front of it before simply rolling over the wire.

0039. Fragos to Captain Willoughby : "I don't know how many but they have tanks out there!"

0039. Captain Willoughby to Fragos: "Where in the hell are they?"

0043. Fragos to Captain Willoughby: "We have two tanks in our wire!"

Sergeant Fragos immediately left the tower to report to Captain Willoughby what he had seen. Willoughby, at his post in the TOC below, was with "Crossbow," the code name for Lieutenant Colonel Schungel. Crossbow instructed Willoughby to stand by in the TOC while he went with Fragos to confirm the sighting. This was a serious turn of events for the Green Beret camp. An attack by enemy armor, never before recorded in the Second Indochina War, was much more serious than just sappers followed up by the infantry penetration-and-exploitation practice of the NVA.

0047. Unknown station (probably Staff Sergeant Brooks or 104 Company): "We've got five tanks on line right at our wire!"

When Crossbow and Fragos came out of the TOC together, there was no question that immediate and heavy antitank action was necessary. Crossbow, seeing the tanks with his own eyes, instructed Willoughby to call for both air and artillery support on the trail from Lang Troai, from where the tanks appeared to have come. He also instructed Willoughby to call for an aircraft to drop flares, and to use parallel channels to both the Khe Sanh combat base and his own headquarters, Company C in Da Nang.

Willoughby, the A-Team commander, now began dashing up and down the steps of the TOC, trying to assess the progress of the battle. He was busy directing artillery-fire adjustments, making tactical decisions regarding his CIDG troops in their defensive positions, and moving them as the situation dictated.

Crossbow left the TOC to form tank-killer teams. Willoughby, until enemy fire had destroyed the stairs of the TOC beyond repair, continued to race up and down in response to radio calls from his men on top of the ground. He needed to see what was happening as well as hear it over the radio net.

0054. Unknown station (probably again Staff Sergeant Brooks or 104 Company): "We've got tanks inside our wire—I said inside our wire!"

0056–0100. Many radio transmissions from all stations. Noise, small-arms fire, and track vehicles.

The tanks that Sergeant Fragos had seen now stopped to engage the defenders of 104 Company. The NVA tanks, which would be the first of eleven that early morning of 7 February, were a version of the Soviet Piavaiuschiij tank/amphibious tank first introduced in

1952. The PT-76 had a welded hull to waterproof it for amphibious warfare, and it weighed over fifteen tons. The 76mm main gun of the tank could fire at a sustained maximum rate of fifteen rounds per minute. It carried forty rounds loaded in the ammunition ready rack. The main gun fired at point-blank range into 104 Company's bunkers and defensive positions. Its 7.62mm machine gun was also blasting away at the surprised defenders.

The PT-76, designed more for reconnaissance than for heavy combat, was this early February morning like Goliath against the Israelites. What the defenders needed was a David. They had him, except he had no slingshot. Crossbow had immediately gone into action, forming tank-killer teams. After all, he had one hundred light antitank weapons (LAWs) available, along with enough brave men to do the job. Sergeant Fragos already had several LAWs by his guard position in the tower, and he went to retrieve them immediately, as they were the closest ones available. Fragos returned with the LAWs. He quickly armed and handed each in turn to Crossbow, who fired each throwaway weapon at the first tank.

The PT-76 could not withstand antitank fire, due to its thin skin of welded steel for amphibious purposes. However, the NVA had added to the tank's defensive strength against such attacks by attaching various types of rigging to its exposed vital areas. NVA tank crewmen used wire mesh, rubber matting, and especially wheel drums secured by wire, with braces across the holes in the centers. All acted as field expedient shields to deflect or prematurely detonate antitank rounds.

0101. Craig in 81mm mortar pit to Captain Willoughby, underground in TOC: "There's one tank on the hill with us and a total of seven tanks in all."

0102. Captain Willoughby to FAC (forward air controller) airborne over camp: "Request air strike or anything else you can give us at coordinates [north and west of camp]."

0103. Captain Willoughby to FAC: "We need Spooky [call sign of AC-47 gunship with Gatling guns and illumination flares] to work the south edge of the perimeter."

In the TOC, Captain Willoughby had Sp4c. Frank Dooms report the tank attack to both Khe Sanh combat base and Company C headquarters at Da Nang.

0109. Captain Willoughby to Jacksonville (call sign of marine artillery at Khe Sanh): "Repeat FFE [fire for effect] number eight [preregistered target number], left 200 and right 200, shifting fires."

0109. Captain Willoughby to Jacksonville: "We have tanks coming up the road. Request fire number five. Keep it working up and down the road [Route 9 to the north of the camp]."

The marines at Khe Sanh thought that the Green Berets had gone crazy, and they asked for confirmation. Dooms replied by radioing directly into the fire-direction control center (FDCC) of the marine artillery at the combat base. S.Sgt. Tom Gagnon on the other end couldn't believe his ears either, and he asked for a confirmation on the report of armor in the wire. Dooms confirmed the report.

Willoughby had his hands full trying to monitor excited calls from the MIKE Forces in the OP west of the camp and from 101 Company on the eastern perimeter. Two tanks were approaching Lang Vei on Route 9 from the east, and four were coming from the direction of Laos, headed east.

0117. Captain Willoughby, underground in TOC, to unknown station (probably Lindewald and Hanna at OP): "How are you doin'? Okay? There are tanks in the wire on the south side of the perimeter."

A frustrated Dooms continued to argue with the disbelieving marines at the combat base. Even when he said he could hear the tank engines backfiring, the marine on the other end of the radio transmission replied that it must have been the generators. Willoughby was heatedly calling for an immediate air strike from the FAC who was patrolling the skies above Lang Vei.

0119. Unknown station to FAC: "You can have all the air you want on 388.1."

0120. Bomber flying overhead to FAC: "Got a B-57 with funny bombs." (These were also known as soft bombs. They were fragmenting explosives, sometimes with variable-time fuses, also known as cluster-bomb units [CBUs]).

0124. FAC (air force Capt. Gerald L. Harrington, one of the two FACs) to Captain Willoughby: "Where do you want the bombs?"

"All over the south side of the hill and along the road."

"Where those flares are?"

"Yes."

"Any friendlies?"

"No."

Captain Harrington was circling the battle scene some twelve hundred feet over the defenders, paying constant attention to both incoming fire from Khe Sanh and the automatic-weapons fire of the attacking North Vietnamese. As he tried to relieve the infantry pressure with air power, he later recalled thinking, "It looks like the Fourth of July down there, with everyone firing Roman candles."

0128. Specialist Fifth Class McMurry and Staff Sergeant Thompson to Captain Willoughby: "Troops are moving up on this position from two directions."

0130. Craig to radio net: "Uh-oh, the POL dump just went up!"

0132. Specialist Fifth Class McMurry or Staff Sergeant Thompson to Captain Willoughby: "I think the enemy is in our old bunkers. Get some HE [high-explosive rounds] in there."

Finally the marine Fire direction control center at Khe Sanh approved an artillery-fire mission, some seventeen precious minutes after it had originally been requested. What the Lang Vei Green Berets did not know was that the marine artillery at Khe Sanh combat base was simultaneously under fire from the big 152mm artillery pieces on Co Roc Mountain. It was a suppression fire delivered in a heavy volume, designed to keep the marines from effectively supporting the Lang Vei camp. The first barrage of marine artillery fire landed in the middle of the already beleaguered camp. With proper adjustments quickly made, the marines' next barrage found its mark among the NVA attackers.

0133. Captain Willoughby to Jacksonville: "Fire . . . [garbled]."

0134. Jacksonville to Captain Willoughby: "What kind of fuse?"

"Oh hell! Mixed quick and delay, I guess."

0135. Specialist Fifth Class McMurry and Staff Sergeant Thompson to Captain Willoughby: "Is anyone firing VT [variable-timed] fuse at us? Get it off! Get the VT fuse off of us!"

Just as the attack started shortly after midnight, Sfc. Bill Craig, who had not quite fallen asleep, found himself jarred into action by a barrage of 152mm rounds. He quickly roused Sp5c. Dan Phillips. Craig shouted, "Grab your gear and let's move! We won't be back here if this is an attack!"

As he left their bunker and jumped into the adjoining 81mm mortar pit, Dan Phillips was carrying his flak jacket and pistol belt. When they arrived in the pit, Craig and Phillips immediately aimed and fired their mortar. Illumination rounds exposed the attackers and HEAT ripped into the oncoming NVA. Their targets were the four tanks moving east on Route 9 and the NVA infantry that was certainly close behind.

As they fired the mortar, their own position came under fire. Phillips and Craig sprayed the NVA infantry with small-arms fire. A number of incoming mortar rounds found the range of their pit, and one exploded on the parapet close enough to knock both of them to the ground. Craig was bleeding from the ears and Phillips from the eyes. The blast dazed and deafened both men, inflicting facial cuts. Seeing their predicament, Staff Sergeant Brooks ran immediately to their assistance from his machine-gun position. He found them conscious. Craig and Phillips soon convinced

Brooks that they could continue to fight, so he returned to his machine gun, and they again began firing the 81.

The situation changed abruptly for Craig and Phillips when a nearby fuel supply exploded. When some of the yet-unburned fuel started to trickle into their position, Craig yelled to Phillips, "Let's get out of here!" Soon after their departure, the gasoline fire reached the 81mm mortar ammo and exploded. Craig and Phillips made their way to the 4.2-inch mortar pit, joining Tiroch, Thompson, and Burke.

IN THE camp at Old Lang Vei, Sgt. Richard Allen tried to get some sleep at about 2300. It had been a bit hectic. He and Sp4c. Joel Johnson had eaten dinner at the new camp as the artillery from Co Roc blasted the Lang Vei camp, impairing Allen's digestion. They had returned to the old camp by jeep. Allen, relaxing over a beer with Ashley, had decided it was time to forget a bad day and prepare for a worse one. About fifteen minutes after midnight, Johnson awakened Allen and informed him that Lang Vei was under attack. Ashley was already on the radio, a PRC-25. The three Green Berets were almost helpless. They had not been able to get the Elephant Battalion's officers to cooperate in anything except chow call.

The three medics heard the calls from Willoughby requesting artillery fire and air strikes. According to Allen, it was almost 0130 before any fire came from Khe Sanh, and that was illumination. Although there was an FAC over the camp, the air support consisted of one Spooky dropping flares, not coming down close enough to use his powerful Gatling guns.

The medics had not been able to get the Laotians to help them. The new camp needed illumination from the Laotian mortars, but none was forthcoming. Ashley had tried unsuccessfully to persuade the Laotian colonel to participate.

Finally, Allen got angry. "I need to talk to the colonel. We need to have illum rounds sent out," he told the burly bodyguard blocking the entrance to Colonel Soulang's underground command bunker.

The bodyguard continued to block the entrance. Allen, a former wrestler, martial-arts instructor, and football player, forced his way past him, knowing that he was breaking a number of laws of military courtesy. He demanded that the colonel have his troops fire illumination rounds over the besieged new camp. "We're being attacked by tanks," the Green Beret said emphatically.

When the colonel again refused, the Green Beret tried another, less diplomatic method of persuasion. He pulled his .45-caliber pistol from his holster and chambered a round.

Soon thereafter the Laotians began dropping the illumination rounds into their 81mm tubes.

Then the NVA armor turned their attention to the Old Lang Vei camp. Tank main guns and machine guns fired at the poorly prepared Laotians as two of the PT-76s entered the drop zone below the old camp. Only Ashley, Johnson, and Allen defended the camp. Johnson, the first to spot the two tanks, asked Ashley for fifty men and a 3.5-inch rocket launcher, promising to knock out both tanks.

Ashley agreed but the Laotian commander did not. Before this disagreement went any further, the two tanks turned their attention back to Lang Vei's new camp. The three Green Berets had only been able to put out a relatively small amount of fire against the tanks, which had hammered the front of the old camp.

Ashley was on the PRC-25, controlling the flare ship and instructing it where to drop the illumination. The clear early evening sky had turned into a night of limited visibility. At about 0330, the Green Berets from the old camp watched as B-52s pounded Co Roc Mountain in Laos, just a few miles away. The old camp lost radio contact with Willoughby in the TOC at about 0420, so Ashley and his two Green Berets directed air strikes against the NVA at the new camp.

FIRST LT. THOMAS E. Todd, the visiting engineer, was in the living quarters at the rear of supply bunker number 1 when the attack began. At 0100 he watched an enemy tank roll past the front of the bunker, heading for the TOC. He quickly returned to his living quarters for a supply of grenades stashed there. But before he reached the grenades, an enemy artillery round scored a direct hit on the bunker. Todd dashed out of the destroyed bunker, heading for the emergency medical bunker nearby.

No sooner had he entered the medical bunker when a passing tank paused to fire a shot from its main gun at the bunker's entrance from point-blank range. The blast was followed by several grenades. Todd could not leave through the rear exit, as another tank fired a round at that door, slightly wounding him. Both tanks pulled away and another appeared, headed for the TOC. This one was closely followed by at least one platoon of NVA infantry. Todd immediately decided that remaining quiet until daylight was the prudent plan for him. He could see only enemy troops in his immediate area and feared that the camp was already in their control.

He quietly observed as tanks moved about the area from about 0230 until 0600, when their activity ceased. By 0630 even the small-arms fire had died down, and he could see enemy troops moving and talking in a noncombat mode. Todd thought he could stay hidden until nightfall and escape in the dark, but he suddenly changed his mind when, at about 0800, American aircraft attacked the camp. The enemy fought back with automatic weapons and small arms.

At about 1400, he saw helicopters circling the camp. This led him to believe that there must still be Green Berets fighting from the TOC. For the next three hours the bombing and strafing increased.

THE A-TEAM executive officer, 1st Lt. Miles R. Wilkins, was in the 4.2-inch mortar pit helping to fire illumination at the beginning of the battle. He then grabbed an LAW and headed for the southwest corner of the camp. Just as he was going into that corner, a number of indigenous troops rushed past him.

"Beaucoup VC, beaucoup VC!" they shouted to Wilkins.

Wilkins went ahead anyway. Suddenly a tank appeared between the bunkers. Ten NVA followed closely

Company C, 5th Special Forces staff and South Vietnamese special forces counterparts, circa August 1967. Lt. Col. Daniel Schungel is in the front row, center. Capt. Frank Willoughby is fifth from right, back row. *Edward T. Damaso*

Lt. Col. Schungel and his Vietnamese counterpart at C Company Headquarters in Da Nang.

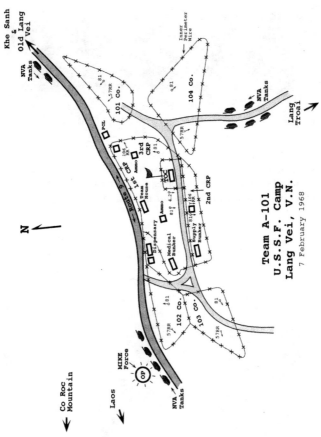

Team A-101
U.S.S.F. Camp
Lang Vei, V.N.

7 February 1968

Old Lang Vei Camp in May 1967. *Edward T. Damaso*

(Opposite page)
Team A-101 U.S. Army Special Forces Camp Lang Vei, Vietnam, 7 February 1968.

First Lt. Paul Longgrear and enlisted men in front of pre-mission "lock–down" building at Fort Bragg, July 1967. Longgrear commanded the MIKE Force at Lang Vei. *Paul Longgrear*

Sp5c. Daniel R. Phillips, missing in action after the Battle of Lang Vei. *William R. Phillips*

MIKE Force platoon leader Sfc. Charles Lindewald was a member of one of the first "A" teams in Vietnam. The tiger's tooth on his necklace was a personal trophy. Lindewald was listed as missing in action after the Battle for Lang Vei. *Paul Longgrear*

A captured Soviet-made PT-76 amphibious tank of the type used by the North Vietnamese Army during the Battle for Lang Vei. The battle marked the first time the North Vietnamese had used armor in an offensive assault against American troops. *U.S. Army Military History Institute*

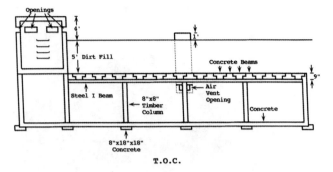

Diagram of the Tactical Operations Center (TOC) at Lang Vei.
U.S. Army After Action Report, 22 March 1968

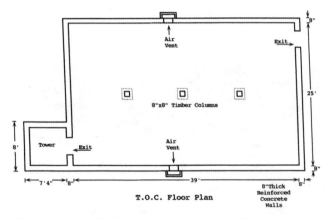

Floor plan of the TOC at Lang Vei. U.S. Army After Action
Report, 22 March 1968

Sfc. Bill Craig and First Lt. Paul Longgrear outside of the hospital in Japan where they were recuperating from wounds received during the Battle of Lang Vei. *Paul Longgrear*

Capt. Frank Willoughby being presented the Silver Star and the Navy Presidential Unit Citation by Lt. Gen. Cushman. *Frank Willoughby*

Lt. Gen. Robert Cushman, USMC, and Lt. Col. Paul Schungel at the awards ceremony for Lang Vei survivors held at C Company Headquarters, 5th Special Forces Group, Da Nang.
Frank Willoughby

behind the tank. To Wilkins, it was like kids playing cowboys and Indians in the woods. As the tank closed to within five meters, Wilkins attempted to fire the LAW. It misfired. Ironically, that was probably to his advantage: Wilkins was close enough that the blast, if the LAW had worked, might have wounded or killed him.

He ran from the tank as green tracers buzzed over his head. Arriving at the north side of the 4.2-inch mortar pit, he observed a tank in the northwest corner, past the dispensary. He had two LAWs. He fired the first and missed. His second shot was on target, hitting near the turret ring. The tank, showing no ill effect, simply cranked its turret to face the direction of the shot. Wilkins remembers deciding that if the LAW was light antitank, this tank was probably a medium.

This was the second time that Wilkins had seen this tank. The first time had been below the team house. He had been looking down on the scene from the roof of the team house and had seen one of the tanks stopped on the road nearby. Four or five of the CIDG troops were climbing on the tank, but they did not seem to know what to do with it. The tank brushed them off and continued down the road.

Soon thereafter he joined Crossbow and Fragos. While Crossbow fired the LAWs that Fragos handed to him, others joined them to help stop the enemy armor. Also in the tank-killer teams with Crossbow and Fragos were Lieutenant Quy (the VNSF operations officer) and Specialist Fifth Class McMurry. The camp's 4.2-inch mortar provided illumination as the teams went into action.

• • •

LIEUTENANT LONGGREAR had had a bad start to his evening on 6 February, when his MIKE Force platoon had initially refused to return to the OP. He had come back to his sleeping bunker below the 81mm mortar pit about fifty meters southeast of the TOC, to try to relax just before dark.

With him was one of his platoon commanders, Sgt. John Early, who was sharing his bunker while his own was being built. They were just about asleep when the radio crackled as the battle began, less than an hour into 7 February.

Unknown station to Sergeant Early in the sleeping bunker:

"We've got enemy tanks in the wire!"

"We've got what? Where?"

Longgrear and Early dashed up the bunker steps to their assigned fighting position, the 81mm mortar right above their sleeping bunker. Since there were no visible targets, they pumped out a number of illumination rounds. The radio request had been urgent. Several hundred NVA accompanied five tanks, and 104 Company needed illumination. Sergeant Thompson soon joined them to form a fire-support team that dropped illumination and HEAT along the wire to the south. Almost thirty minutes passed before the team finally saw the first tank. Two more rolled into view. Surprisingly, the tanks did not appear to have the infantry that would normally be present to protect the armor from the camp's defenders. Longgrear remembers thinking,

"Good. The indigenous troops and the mortars were doing their job."

Lieutenant Longgrear sent his two men down into the bunker below their mortar pit to retrieve the fifteen LAWs stashed there. Meanwhile he attempted to drop some HEAT right on the tank turrets. Thompson and Early returned with the LAWs. Longgrear saw a tank amid the reddish-orange and green tracers burning through the dark and fog. It was heading directly toward the inner perimeter and his mortar pit. He armed an LAW and aimed at the tank. The LAW failed to fire when he squeezed the rubber triggering mechanism. Early passed him another LAW. Again it failed to fire. This time Thompson handed him one, with the same result. Longgrear rearmed it and tried again. Now it fired, but when it struck the armor of the tank, which it should have penetrated easily, it simply glanced off at an upward angle. None of the three tank killers could believe the results.

The three split up as the tank approached their mortar pit, firing its 76mm main gun. Longgrear dispatched Sergeant Early to his platoon area to help the others. He sent Sergeant Thompson to assist Sergeant First Class Brande and his platoon, heavily engaged with the enemy. Lieutenant Longgrear decided to try his luck by attacking the tank from its more vulnerable flank, and the move proved successful, as he knocked out his first tank. He joined Crossbow at this stage.

It was several minutes before one in the morning. Sfc. James Holt and Sfc. Earl Burke manned the only 106mm recoilless rifle in action at the time. Holt directed very effective fire on the tanks approaching the camp from the Lang Troai trail. NVA infantry and tanks penetrated 104 Company, and the CIDG there were in deep trouble. The tanks were decimating the CIDG on the southern perimeter with close-range firepower and infantry assault by some five hundred NVA. Holt was successful in knocking out two of the tanks while they were still in the wire. Willoughby had left the TOC momentarily and saw Holt blow the turret completely off the second tank. Two other tanks clanked around the knocked-out, burning hulks of the first two, completely penetrated the defensive wire, and were heading directly at Crossbow and Longgrear. It took at least five hits from LAWs to disable the one most directly threatening them. A shower of orange sparks indicated each had been hit by an LAW, but it was almost as if the LAW round was traveling at half-speed and therefore not delivering its normal lethal blow.

When the LAWs had finally destroyed the tank, the three crewmen grabbed their AK-47s and crawled out to avoid being burned to death. Crossbow and Lieutenant Quy killed all three with small-arms fire and grenades. The second tank maneuvered its way around the knocked-out tank to continue the attack and help exploit the penetration of the camp's inner perimeter. It was firing at Schungel's tank-killer team with both the main gun and the 7.62mm machine gun from a distance of about thirty meters. Crossbow had set up his team behind some rock-filled fifty-five-gallon drums just outside the TOC. Lieutenant Longgrear engaged and killed four sappers before Schungel dispatched him down the stairs to the TOC to bring back more LAWs and hand grenades. Lieutenant Wilkins had just joined them.

Crossbow was throwing grenades at the oncoming tank. "I can't seem to hit it," he yelled to Wilkins. Wilkins then threw a grenade that got under the front track of the tank, but it kept coming, closing to within twenty meters. The 76mm main gun of the NVA tank concentrated fire on the drums, destroying the tank-killer team's cover and at the same time blasting the TOC entrance and destroying the stairs.

Lieutenant Longgrear saw the blast that destroyed drums protecting Lieutenant Colonel Schungel and several others. Convinced that Crossbow had been killed, Longgrear reported the demise of their brave commanding officer to Captain Willoughby. Schungel had repeatedly exposed himself to deadly fire in trying to knock out the tanks.

Of the four men who had been with Schungel at the time of the blast, only Lieutenant Quy had escaped a wound. Schungel later said that Lieutenant Quy's continuous stream of small-arms fire was the only thing that saved his team from certain death by the NVA infantry trying to outflank them.

Schungel, in the midst of the already chaotic situation, saw that several tanks had penetrated the western perimeter.

Tank-killer teams quickly formed there. Green Beret Dan Phillips, already wounded but still fighting, grabbed as many LAWs and grenades as he could carry and faced down one of the tanks. Phillips fired the LAWs as the blasts from the tank's main gun and machine gun fired at him from nearly point-blank range. Because the LAWs were not firing effectively, Phillips wanted to get as close as he could. This maneuver must have startled the tank crew, as they missed him repeatedly. He and the others fired again and again, finally destroying the armored behemoth. By this time Phillips had completely expended his ammunition, and with enemy rounds hitting all around him, he escaped to a backup defensive position to continue the fight.

At this point many stations began transmitting, at times cutting each other out.

0136. FAC to Captain Willoughby, underground in TOC: "We've got two F-100s with 750-pounders on standby."

0136. Sgt. Richard H. Allen at Old Lang Vei to radio net: "Christ, a bomb just fell on our position!"

0136. Sgt. Earl F. Burke to radio net: "There are two tanks on the main road [Route 9] by the mess hall on the road to Khe Sanh."

0136. Unknown station to radio net: "Can you get the LAW over here?" "We don't have any more LAWs left."

After the NVA tank's main gun destroyed the defensive position of Schungel's team behind the rock-filled barrels, First Lieutenant Wilkins, crushed between several of the heavy barrels, was unconscious. Specialist Fifth Class McMurry, blinded by the blast and with hands mangled by the shrapnel, was in serious condition. Schungel, thrown into the air by the blast impact, had only a slight wound in the right hip and a lacerated left cheek and ear. The barrels that team sergeant Craig had ordered filled with rocks had served their purpose.

It is sometimes amazing what simple materials can do in a sophisticated age of supertechnical weaponry. There were times that combat in Vietnam, especially in the Hill Fights, came down to bare fists and entrenching tools being smashed against the face and head of the enemy. Modern warfare sometimes—although perhaps rarely—becomes a brawl with no holds barred.

0145. FAC to Captain Willoughby: "Where do you want that fire?"

"All over the area."

0150. FAC to Jacksonville: "Fire the preplanned fires right on his position."

0151. FAC to bomber: "I want you to put those hard bombs [conventional nonfragmenting explosives] to the east of the camp entrance right on the road. Jacksonville, 06 [Willoughby] wants you to keep those flares coming!"

0157. FAC to Craig: "I've got one more bomb. Where do you want it?"

0200. Captain Willoughby to Craig: "I think we got a tank down by the dispensary. There is another by supply. We didn't get it. There's one by supply."

0208. FAC to Craig: "I only have soft bombs. They spread out. Do you want them on the eastern end?"

0209. FAC to Spooky: "Put your fire on the eastern end of the perimeter."

0209. Craig to FAC: "We have a very active tank on each end of the perimeter."

0210. Craig to FAC: "Tanks and a lot of infantry are coming into the camp!"

0215. Craig to FAC: "They are coming in from each end of the camp. We will have to do something soon!"

0216. Jacksonville to FAC: "Can we help?"

0216. FAC to Craig: "Can Jacksonville help?"

"Yes! Flares! Flares! Flares!"

0218. Craig to FAC: "There are more tanks coming! We've got to do something!"

0220. FAC to Craig: "We've got bombs. Do you want them on the eastern end of your position?"

0221. Craig to Captain Willoughby: "Those tanks are tearing up 104 Company!"

0222. FAC to Craig: "Fighters are coming down to take a look at it now."

0223. Craig to Captain Willoughby: "Tanks coming our way!"

0225. FAC to second FAC: "I'm out of rockets. Can you mark the trail at the east entrance of the camp?"

"Let me get oriented and I think I can get it."

0227. Craig to FAC: "There is a tank coming up on the TOC!"

0230. Craig to Captain Willoughby to FAC: "There is a tank right on top of the TOC and it's giving us fits! We knocked one out."

0230–0238. FAC attempts to contact Craig and Willoughby.

0238. FAC to Craig: "Do you want us to put something on that tank?"

"No!"

0239–0245. FAC cannot contact any element at Lang Vei.

0245. FAC to Craig: "Where do you want the bombs?"

"Put the bombs just south of the green star cluster to get the tank. We're moving off the hill."

This was the last transmission monitored from any station in Lang Vei camp by outside radio operators. Company C monitored the transmissions of Sfc. Eugene Ashley and the two medics with him at the Old Lang Vei camp as late as 0250. Frank Willoughby remembers that other calls were made, perhaps not monitored.

The situation inside the TOC had begun to deteriorate. The tank that had destroyed the barrels protecting Lieutenant Colonel Schungel's tank-killer team had also destroyed the main entrance to the TOC. The second entrance, a seldom-used emergency exit, was in the tower. Two tanks were firing at both entrances to the TOC and using the tower as a target, from a distance of less than fifteen meters. One round seriously wounded both Sergeant Early and Specialist Fourth Class Moreland, who had gone to the top of the TOC tower to retrieve an M-60 machine gun. Early's legs were nearly useless and Moreland suffered a terrible head wound, but others brought both men down from the tower into the TOC and treated them.

Captain Willoughby by this time had no idea if any Green Berets were alive in the camp above him. He could not get out of the TOC, and they could not get in to him without knocking out the tanks. Jets flew overhead, but the illumination, which by now was all coming from Khe Sanh and Spooky, was insufficient to provide targets for air support.

In the TOC with Willoughby were Lieutenant Longgrear, S.Sgt. Emanuel Phillips, Staff Sergeant Brooks, Sergeant Early, Specialist Fourth Class Moreland, Sergeant Fragos, and Specialist Fourth Class Dooms. Also there were the VNSF camp commander, 104 Company commander, Willoughby's interpreter, a CIDG communications specialist, and approximately a dozen other indigenous personnel.

One of the fifteen-ton tanks had rolled onto the top of the TOC in a futile attempt to crush it. NVA sappers were doing their best to destroy the seemingly impervious bunker. Satchel charges came flying down the main entrance and tower. Continuous attempts by the NVA with the charges and with grenades still could not force the surrender of the Green Berets in the TOC.

It was at about this time that Captain Willoughby remembers calling Jacksonville at Khe Sanh and asking them to place an artillery barrage directly on his position, as well as asking the marines to execute the rescue orders. As he tells the story, Willoughby was informed that there would be no relief force sent in; they had been written off.

Captain Willoughby was furious: the marines had a mission to come to the rescue of the camp, if needed. Willoughby knew from the radio reports that the NVA controlled his camp. His situation was desperate, and, if they had been officially written off, there was no hope.

In fairness to the marine decision not to effect the rescue attempt, the certainty of ambush ruled out the fastest overland route, along Route 9. The route through the bush would take far too long and would also be met with ambushes. The helicopters could not land troops at Lang Vei camp while it was under attack, with tanks sitting in wait on the landing zones. Rescue was just not feasible, even though the designated marine units were champing at the bit.

News of the rescue request and its denial by the marines soon reached the commander of all the Special Forces in Vietnam, Col. Jonathan F. Ladd. Ladd was furious. He called Saigon immediately, demanding to speak directly with the commander of all U.S. forces in Vietnam, Gen. William C. Westmoreland. General Westmoreland, awakened, assessed the situation and replied that he could not overrule the decision of the commander who was actually on the ground. Westmoreland did authorize the use of Firecracker, the code name for COFRAM, a secret new weapon. Fired by an artillery piece, Firecracker appeared to land like a dud. Instead, it scattered hundreds of small grenade-type explosives that then went off, covering a wide area with man killers. At first the Lang Vei defenders were concerned that its use might impair their air support, which was vital. After several radio messages to this effect, plus reports to Khe Sanh that the enemy controlled the camp above ground level, Maj. Gen. Rathvon Tompkins made the tough decision. Tompkins, commanding the Third Marine Division, ordered an alternating program of COFRAM followed by HEAT and VT artillery shells and then air strikes.

The marine artillery fired COFRAM three times. Shortly after 0230 the TOC had lost all radio contact. The next radio contact for the TOC would be with Old Lang Vei, several hours later. For the next six to seven hours, the TOC was out of radio contact. Grenades and satchel charges blasted the battered shelter. The grenades used were fragmentation, thermite, white phosphorus, and tear gas. Paul Longgrear gives this account of hell in the TOC:

The most excruciating part of the whole time in the TOC was the hours I spent with my back to the wall where they were digging. Tap, tap, tap, for several hours. When they finally blew in the wall, the hole was only about two feet from where I'd been sitting. The only reason I moved was to get a better shot against them coming down the escape hatch in the tower. One of the frag grenades they dropped got me in the ankle, but I never loosened my boot, and that helped. We sat there in pure darkness. It was tough to keep the indige [indigenous troops] from talking or moving. In the dark, I worried that one of them might be trying to kill me, reaching to find my throat with a knife. I knew that if we made it to daylight, we'd be okay.

At about 0300 a burst from an NVA flamethrower spit fire down the tower and started a blaze that the Green Berets put out after fighting it for about twenty minutes. Fortunately the fire had not spread. Willoughby remembers that the NVA tried to use a flamethrower down through the TOC tower. A buffer wall in the superbly engineered and built reinforced concrete fortress absorbed the blast of fire and protected the besieged defenders. With the flamethrower, the NVA also used tear-gas grenades. These lasted longer, due to the lack of ventilation that had helped contain the fire. The trapped men shared the available gas masks. Moreland gave Longgrear an NVA gas mask; someone else gave him a helmet to wear, which he had never done before in combat. "It must have been Willoughby," he recalls, "because I put it on."

Those without gas masks kept their heads as close to the floor as possible. At about 0330, the sappers who were on top of the TOC called down the tower in Vietnamese, saying that they were about to blow up the bunker and inviting its defenders to surrender. The indigenous personnel had been able to survive this far, but they decided it was time to surrender, without telling the Green Berets. The Green Berets initially thought—erroneously—that the indigenous troops were trying to break out of the TOC and fight their way to safety. Lieutenant Longgrear went to the door to lead the Americans out.

As the indigenous personnel found their way in the darkness up the battered and nearly nonexistent stairs, a stunned Longgrear watched from the doorway. "They are surrendering! They are giving up!" Longgrear yelled to the other Green Berets, who were making preparations for a breakout.

The CIDG and the Vietnamese, rifles held high above their heads as they warily attempted to negotiate their way to ground level from the smoky hell of the TOC, had had enough. By the light of the flares still providing sporadic illumination, Longgrear could see the NVA soldier at the top of the passageway, and he remembers thinking about shooting him.

He also remembers other thoughts racing through his mind. There was the Easter Sunday spent in jail at age seventeen, when he had promised himself never again to be confined. There was the TV in his grandmother's living room, where, at age ten, he had watched the release of American POWs after horrendous captivity during the Korean War. As they walked across the bridge at Panmunjom, Longgrear recalls the tears that burned his eyes and his vow never to be captured. There was no surrender in this man, nor in any of the other Green Berets trapped in this hell.

Unconfirmed later reports stated that the captors

stripped the prisoners down to their shorts and confiscated their weapons. Shots from an AK-47 allegedly then rang out, followed by more in close order. Some thought the NVA had summarily executed many or all of the captives. However, neither Willoughby nor Longgrear can confirm these reports of the alleged executions.

From inside the bunker, the Green Berets, determined to fight to the death, assumed positions against the assault that would surely follow. They could hear bombs, artillery fire, and low-flying aircraft. Willoughby remembers calling in everything the Americans and South Vietnamese could muster. The "Spad" (nicknamed for the World War I fighter plane) of the Second Indochina War, the Douglas Skyraider A-1E, dropped 250-pound bombs and napalm. These "slow movers" then strafed targets of opportunity and headed back to their air bases or carriers to reload, refuel, and do it again. NVA ground fire brought down one South Vietnamese A-1E. There were also A-4Ds and F-8U Crusaders in the fray. The air strikes continued.

Longgrear recalls grabbing at what he believed would be his final minutes alive. For the first time in his life, he attempted to communicate with his creator. Proud to the end, he felt that he was doing all this for the sake of his family, for Patty and the baby. It was on their behalf that he now spoke privately to God, reminding Him that his wife was a good Christian woman and asking Him to watch over Patty and Honey Lee after his demise. The hard-case lieutenant was not going to call on the Lord to help him: he would die as he had lived, unsaved.

As the radio operators struggled with the PRC-74 to regain contact with Old Lang Vei after losing it twice, Willoughby worried about his men. He knew nothing of those outside the TOC. His last radio contact had been from Sergeant Tiroch, Craig's radio operator. That had been at about 0230, when Tiroch had reported that he had only one round left with tanks headed right at him.

Just before 0500, the tapping sound stopped, after what seemed to the Green Berets like many hours. The noise had been made by the sappers, driving a shape charge deep into the ground. Now they plugged the shape charge at both ends, so that its full force would blast the wall along the north side of the TOC. It was obvious to them that their grenades and satchel charges were having little or no effect on the well-built bunker. The shape charge, placed six or seven feet deep, was close to the air vent.

The work was effective. They blew out a portion of the north wall about six feet wide and four feet high. The force of the explosion blew Longgrear up against the far wall, ripping his watch off his wrist. The helmet saved his life. A chunk of concrete from the imploding wall dented the helmet and tore into his head. Later it would require over a dozen stitches to close the wound.

The blast worsened Moreland's already deteriorating condition, and unless he got immediate surgery, he was not long for this world. He was delirious. The blast knocked all of the TOC defenders unconscious, except Fragos. He continued single-handedly to defend the TOC. *Newsweek* magazine reported the following conversation in its 19 February 1968 issue. A voice from above the ground spoke in English.

"Are you there?" the NVA asked the TOC inhabitants.

"Yes, I'm here," answered Fragos.

"Have you got a weapon?"

"Yep."

"Have you ammunition?"

"I've got plenty for you."

Longgrear was the first to regain consciousness. He recalls lying flat on his back on the floor, covered with a large piece of the former plywood wall. He heard feet shuffling across the floor but could not see anything, because of the plywood on top of him. He could only imagine that it was the enemy bayoneting the wounded. Looking out from the edge of the plywood, he saw daylight through the hole in the wall. He did not know where he was. When he heard the shuffling feet again, he eased his right hand slowly above his head, searching carefully for his weapon. When he found the CAR-15 handle, he eased it down toward the middle of his stomach. Moving his hand over it, Longgrear deemed the weapon to be intact. He released the safety. Throwing off the plywood with his left arm, Longgrear jumped to his feet with a yell and found himself facing down Fragos, with both of them about to shoot the other at point-blank range.

They went to each of the others, reviving them. They had to slap several to bring them back to consciousness. As the others again resumed fighting positions, Longgrear leaned Moreland up against the wall and placed a rifle in his lap, with the hope that he would be able to die fighting if the NVA came through the TOC entrance. If they came in, Longgrear knew that Moreland would want to kill as many as he could before he died.

He told Moreland, "Don't shoot anybody unless the NVA come in."

The hole caused by the blast provided an entrance for fragmentation grenades. The explosion had not only knocked seven of the eight Green Berets unconscious, it had wounded all of them. The situation was deteriorating still more. The shrapnel from one grenade wounded Willoughby shortly after 0700. He suffered nine wounds to his head alone. Sp4c. Franklin Dooms gave him a morphine injection. "I don't think that worked," Willoughby recalls Dooms saying after the first injection into his leg, "I'll try another one." Willoughby finally lost consciousness at about 0800. Dooms also applied a first-aid packet around Brooks's head.

DURING A very brief lull, Lieutenant Colonel Schungel was able to assist McMurry to a sandbagged position where he would be more comfortable. Wilkins remembers getting hit: "I felt like it stung me. I remember being down on all fours like I was crawling, except I couldn't move. I had heard Schungel say to McMurry, 'I think Wilkins has had it.'"

Even so, Crossbow checked again. By the time Crossbow got to the lieutenant, Wilkins was just starting to regain consciousness. Wilkins tried his best to stand but only got as far as his hands and knees. Schungel helped the wounded lieutenant get better situated and returned momentarily to their defense.

Lieutenant Quy, after agreeing with Schungel that they would be better off in a shell hole until first light, became separated from the colonel as another tank approached them from the rear. Schungel threw two grenades under it, just as it took another hit from the rear; Schungel judged it to be an LAW. The tank exploded. The hatch blew open but no crewmen appeared. The combination of two grenades under it and an LAW hitting it from the rear, where infantry should have protected it, was too much for this PT-76. Fire billowed from the open hatch. Schungel estimated the time of this kill to be about 0300.

Meanwhile, the NVA in their green uniforms and steel helmets were overrunning the camp. Lieutenant Colonel Schungel and Lieutenant Wilkins, now fully conscious, decided first to go down to the TOC. They then changed their minds, being of the same opinion that team sergeant Bill Craig had preached: a bunker leaves little room for fire and maneuver. Instead they crept down to the team house. Schungel helped Wilkins take a position behind the unfinished bar, while he took a more central position where he could observe both doors. He cut the inner-tube door returns so that both doors would stand open.

Flares continued to go off as more NVA approached the inner perimeter. Schungel could see fairly well. He did not like what he saw at about half past three in the morning. Five NVA approached the team house, three armed with AK-47s and two bearing satchel charges. Luckily for Crossbow, still David to the NVA Goliath, the five bunched tightly together. He had only two magazines left, and two grenades. He sprayed all five NVA with one magazine. Then another group set off a satchel charge on the team house and raked it with small-arms fire. Schungel, wounded again, this time in the right lower leg, was still able to walk. He moved quietly back to Wilkins, who had lost his weapon in the blast against the oil-drum barricade, and briefed him. Crossbow felt it was best to get out of the team house while they still could. Wilkins was improving somewhat and was lucid enough to recommend that they take cover under the dispensary just over one hundred meters to the west. (Today, Wilkins does not remember even being in the team house.) Silently they made their way there. It was now about 0430. While they remained under the dispensary, an NVA platoon was in the building for a time, ransacking it and then leaving before daylight.

7

Escape and Counterattack

While the cat-and-mouse game between Crossbow, Wilkins, and the NVA continued, team sergeant Craig and Staff Sergeant Tiroch, along with about fifty CIDG, fought fiercely against superior numbers and firepower of the NVA, which forced them toward the northeastern section of the perimeter. They weaved their way through the inner wire and headed toward the Old Lang Vei camp. Several other Green Berets, including Dan Phillips, had also found their way through the wire. Craig last saw Dan Phillips when he and another Green Beret (whom Craig believes was Burke) went through the tanglefoot inner wire and were wending their way through the triple concertina outer wire. They were trapped in a cross fire between two tanks but appeared to be safe, as Craig thought the tanks were firing too high to hit either of them.

Next it was Craig, Tiroch, Thompson, and Brande who would go through the wire. Even though they knew the location of the mines and trip flares, this was no stroll through the park. They were under fire, trying to avoid mines and booby traps, and operating under light provided by parachute flares. Often it was light when they wanted it dark, and dark when they needed to see. The northern perimeter was the only real choice they had for escape, as they could not see any activity there. They knew that the tanks were literally on top of the TOC and had no idea of the situation there, as they had previously lost radio contact.

The group made it successfully through the inner wire. Just as they attempted to penetrate the triple concertina of the outer perimeter, the enemy discovered them and opened fire with heavy machine guns from the eastern penetration. Craig and Tiroch, as well as about ten of the CIDG, were still inside the concertina. The illumination appeared when they least needed it. Spooky and the artillery were doing their job according to their last instructions, which had been to provide illumination so that the defenders could see the attackers coming. Craig and Tiroch dived into some shallow ditches for the five minutes that the artificial illumination brightened the sky. The two Green Berets then dashed for the cover of some bamboo about one hundred meters away.

The Green Berets and the CIDG still with them suffered from American help. Cluster-bomb units burst around them, fragments slightly wounding both Tiroch and Craig and at least one CIDG. The CIDG then apparently decided that they had had enough, and they left Tiroch and Craig behind. The two Green Berets moved forward one hundred meters or more, to the scant protection of a dry creek bed where they spent the remainder of the darkness.

• • •

JUST BEFORE dawn the three medics had another problem, when the people in Lang Vei village tried to get into the Laotian camp. It became necessary to persuade the Laotian colonel to remove them. After that they received more unwelcome news: the FAC reported NVA heading toward the old camp and village.

At first light the three medics went to Lieutenant Colonel Soulang and requested help to attack the NVA at the new camp. This time he allowed them to take volunteers. It took an hour to round up a hundred Laotian soldiers to face an enemy who obviously controlled the high ground of the new camp. It would be an uphill struggle in more ways than one. At about 0645, the old camp heard from the TOC. Ashley told the besieged Green Berets that he and his men were organizing a counterattack.

The NVA were in the defensive positions vacated by the CIDG. Ashley's relief column met about twenty CIDG and MIKE Force Hre just outside the Old Lang Vei camp on Route 9. He persuaded them to join his force to help relieve the pressure on the TOC and perhaps retake the camp. Just before they entered the besieged camp, Ashley called in strafing runs by the two A-4D Skyhawks flying overhead.

As they reached the front gate of the new camp, they spread out to commence the attack up the hill toward the TOC. In the 101 Company area, they found a few seriously wounded CIDG and MIKE Force mercenaries, plus the bodies of two CIDG and several NVA. Satchel charges littered the area.

Allen's carbine jammed at a most inopportune time. There was no time to clear the jam. In order to keep the enemy from later picking it up and using it, he bent the barrel on the side of a bunker and threw it away. From a fallen montagnard, Sergeant Allen picked up a .30-caliber BAR (Browning automatic rifle), all the ammunition he could carry, and some grenades.

As they were about to engage the enemy, suddenly Allen thought of a TV commercial from his youth: in black and white, he saw the Colgate Kid fighting off Mr. Tooth Decay with an invisible plastic shield. After that, Allen did not believe he would die that day. He was right: thanks to his invisible plastic shield, he was the only one of the extracted Green Berets who did not collect a Purple Heart in the battle.

As the counterattacking force entered the 101 Company area, they came under machine-gun fire. The three Green Berets spread out to try to maintain control and discipline of their ragtag line of skirmishers. Ashley took the center and sent Allen to the right flank, Johnson to the left. But before the advance had begun to get under way, the indigenous troops broke and ran. Two NVA machine guns on the left, as well as small-arms fire, pinned down Johnson. A mortar round exploded near enough to him to blow him behind some cover. Johnson saw Allen exposed on the right and called to him to pull back, which they both did in a hurry while Ashley called in air strikes and tried to maintain the line. Ashley assembled the remaining troops while Allen chased those who had run, who were heading back to the camp at Old Lang Vei. While some of the Laotians disappeared, six others returned to the fray with a large and angry Green Beret sergeant pointing his BAR at them.

As DAWN broke, Craig and Tiroch could still hear sporadic firing. Hoping that parts of the camp were still fighting, they decided to move to a position where they could observe the camp without being seen. They spotted an extremely familiar-looking huge black man in tiger stripes—it was Sfc. Eugene Ashley from Old Lang Vei, talking to a group of soldiers.

Craig and Tiroch left their cover just north of Route 9, waving their hands. The Green Berets feared they had walked into a trap when they saw some of the troops wearing NVA caps and carrying AK-47s, but their heartbeats steadied as they saw others with camouflaged uniforms, U.S. carbines, and BARs. The troops with Ashley were members of the Laotian Battalion from Old Lang Vei.

Craig and Tiroch joined them, assisting Ashley as he readied the indigenous troops for a second attack. Craig had a noticeable hip wound and had still not fully regained his hearing from the previous night's concussion wound. Ashley sent Allen to join Tiroch on one flank. The old war horse Craig teamed up with Johnson on the other.

On the first assault, the Green Berets had tried to pinpoint the enemy positions. Allen himself had identified at least nine NVA defending the hill, occupying the former 101 Company bunkers. This time the force led by Ashley found both 81mm and 60mm mortar rounds playing a deadly tune around them. When Allen was only about twenty-five feet from the first enemy bunker, the counterattackers were the targets for grenades coming down the hill at them. The machine-gun fire was intense, about waist high. Allen was hugging the earth under him, protected only by a clump of dirt. The BAR had the firepower that had earned it its reputation in World War II and Korea. A BAR man's life expectancy was extremely short.

ALLEN OPENED up on the enemy positions. They could hear him but could not quite see him; he was barely out of view. Finally they located him, and a horror-stricken Green Beret watched one of the baseball-type American fragmentation hand grenades roll right at him. It stopped just an arm's length away, in full view of his bulging eyeballs. As Allen told himself this was going to hurt, the grenade, incredibly, failed to explode. Promptly he scurried away in a rapid low crawl, before the grenade changed its mind.

At this point the indigenous troops again withdrew in haste, and the five Green Berets again tried to round up the strays and resume the attack. During the second withdrawal, a number of wounded CIDG saw their chance to reach safety and bolted down the hill. The medics quickly tended to the wounded, bandaging as many as they could and injecting morphine into the more seriously wounded.

Regrouping once more, the attack force paused to allow the air strikes and strafing to pin down their adversaries in the bunkers in front of them. Two Green Berets had to force a wounded and exhausted Bill Craig to stay behind. The fighting line was thinner than ever, as over half of the indigenous troops were gone. It was time for the third assault. Ashley needed more firepower. He sent Tiroch and Johnson to find an operational 60mm mortar, which they did and started countermortar fire. The two tried to suppress the enemy fire until their mortar became inoperable. They then picked up their weapons and joined the assault, which once more came close to success without achieving it. The attack seemed to stall. The air support had moved to the other end of the camp, making bombing runs on the NVA infantry and the tanks that were still there. Back down the hill they went.

Ashley had radioed to the old camp to send a 57mm recoilless rifle. Johnson went back to meet the Laotian gunner, and he showed him the two bunkers he wanted targeted on the fourth assault. But the first shot was so high that it went over the top of the camp, and Johnson relieved the Laotian gunner of his 57mm recoilless. He had a man load for him and prepared to fire. On the fourth assault, Johnson knocked out the first bunker with three well-placed rounds. He also put three more in the second bunker, but still the advance was in vain. There was no fire coming from the bunkers, but the indigenous troops refused to advance. Back down the hill they went again.

At about 1050, Ashley radioed to the operator underground in the TOC: "We are about to make an assault through 101 Company's area toward the TOC. Be prepared on my order to assault the NVA from the rear when they turn their attention on our assault."

Ashley now regrouped his men for their fifth assault. This time he asked for close air support just ahead of his advancing troops. Three choppers whirled in, spraying the NVA positions.

Thinking of their conversation about Ashley's family the previous evening, Allen told Ashley, "Stay behind me this time. I've got nothing to lose. You do." Ashley assumed a position one step behind and one step to Allen's right as they again moved up the hill. The assault wave was not receiving any fire from the enemy positions in front of them, but they continued to fire at the NVA positions.

As the assault reached the first enemy position, Allen fired the last round of the BAR's twenty-round magazine. Just as he bent over to change magazines, a burst of AK-47 rounds buzzed past him and hit Ashley, who went down in a heap. Allen immediately turned to his friend, reacting as the trained medic he was and switching gears from being a life taker to a lifesaver.

The AK-47 rounds had torn a hole through the right side of Ashley's chest, through his back, and through the radio he had been carrying on his back. Allen recognized the severity of the sucking chest wound and rendered first aid. He performed mouth-to-mouth resuscitation after placing the plastic bandage from the field dressing packet over the hole in Ashley's back. Then, adrenaline flowing, Allen picked up the limp body of the 220-pound Ashley and ran down the hill carrying him, the BAR, the radio, and Ashley's rifle. Staff Sergeant Tiroch covered Allen's downhill movement with all the fire he could muster, since by this time the choppers who had given covering fire on this fifth assault had left.

Allen ran until his legs would go no more. A Laotian

soldier helped him make a poncho stretcher, and the
two carried and dragged Ashley to the bottom of the
hill. After running down some CIDG and attempting
an unsuccessful flank attack on the left, Johnson heard
that an American was down and raced to the scene.
He helped Tiroch provide cover for Allen as he and the
Laotian soldier dragged Ashley. When he reached the
wire, Allen got several more Laotians to help load Ashley into the back of a jeep they found on the road. With
Allen driving, Johnson gave Ashley artificial resuscitation until they reached the camp at Old Lang Vei.

Meanwhile, as soon as Ashley fell and Allen went to
his aid, the rest of the attackers lost their momentum
and the NVA fire increased. It was just before 1100,
and the last effort to rescue the besieged Green Berets
in the TOC had failed. These counterattacks were typical of the fierce loyalty that the Green Berets had for
one another. Even though the five assaults had failed,
they had diverted the attention of the enemy, undoubtedly keeping the men in the TOC alive.

The jeep bounced down Route 9 and into the old
camp. Allen stopped as they approached a stash of
medical supplies. "Go and get a bottle of D5W [dex-
trose]!" he yelled to Johnson. Allen got some bandages, and Johnson had no sooner left the jeep when
Allen heard the unmistakable sound of incoming artillery fire. Allen was on the driver's side of the jeep.
Quickly he slid under the vehicle just as the 105mm
round hit within ten to fifteen meters of the jeep. A
piece of shrapnel landed harmlessly just inches away
from his left wrist, but the round landed close enough
to kill Ashley and knock Johnson unconscious. Allen

scrambled out from under the jeep and immediately
went to work on Johnson, whose heart had stopped. He
performed an external cardiac massage and mouth-to-
mouth resuscitation until he revived Johnson, but the
blast had taken the last life out of the gallant Ashley.
Sfc. Eugene Ashley, Jr., had demonstrated leadership
and bravery so far above and beyond the call of duty
that he posthumously received his nation's highest decoration, the Medal of Honor.

AT ABOUT 0700, daylight brought air support. However, the ground fire around the dispensary that was
providing a hiding place for Lieutenant Colonel
Schungel and Lieutenant Wilkins, both wounded, was
still too heavy for them to attempt an escape. Approximately two and a half hours later, events determined
their decision to leave. Miles Wilkins remembers
vividly the reason he and Schungel deserted their protected spot under the dispensary.

A fixed-wing aircraft with 20mm wing guns began
strafing very close to the dispensary, slightly wounding
Wilkins in the leg and calf. A number of five-gallon
cans of insect spray sat just outside the dispensary, and
Schungel, concerned that the 20mm fire would hit the
cans and start a fire, did not want to die underneath the
dispensary. The threat prompted them to leave immediately.

The two were able to crawl out from under the building and hobble toward safety. Schungel saw an FAC
overhead and waved to him. The FAC, recognizing the
man on the ground as a Green Beret, waggled his wings

in recognition. At this time, Schungel had no idea if he and Wilkins were the only two Americans still alive at Lang Vei. Because both were barely able to walk, they tried to start every vehicle they encountered as they tried to move quietly from the camp. They had no success.

They next encountered several indigenous forces who had survived the still-ongoing battle, and one tried to help them to his bunker. They immediately received enemy fire. Schungel suffered still another wound, this time in the upper right leg, knocking him to the ground. Wilkins made it safely to the bunker without being hit.

Schungel and Wilkins exited to the north, following the curving road. There was a bunker on the north side of the road. Wilkins, standing beside Schungel, had picked up a stick that he was using as a cane to support his wounded leg. As they approached the bunker, Schungel yelled in to see if anyone was inside. When there was no answer, he tossed in a hand grenade. The two men continued down the road and headed to the old camp, the designated rendezvous point in case of disaster. From their vantage point, they could see activity in the old camp.

Wilkins, slowed by his wounded leg, was following about a hundred meters behind Schungel. He saw an American aircraft coming down the road right at him, its 20mm wing guns blazing. It was a fixed-wing slow mover. The pilot did not recognize Wilkins as a friendly. This is Wilkins's most graphic recollection. "I can remember the little puffs of dirt coming right down the road in front of me. 'This is just like a World War II movie!' I told myself. My next recollection is that I was below the road in an open bunker, so I must have just vaulted off the road. When I finally made it to the old camp, one of the guys [Allen] told me that the colonel said that I'd had it." That was the second time that morning that Crossbow had thought the young lieutenant was dead. Apparently, Wilkins disagreed.

A Vietnamese Special Forces trooper came to Schungel's aid and helped him to the gate and Route 9. Team sergeant Bill Craig saw Schungel and, despite his own wounds, assisted his colonel to the Laotian Battalion command post at Old Lang Vei, where both received first aid for their wounds.

After his wounds had been treated, Lieutenant Colonel Schungel operated the radio and coordinated the efforts of the FAC in providing air cover to the TOC and the men still trapped there.

At about 0900, the TOC finally regained radio contact with team sergeant Craig in the Laotian command post at Old Lang Vei. The TOC also reestablished radio contact with the FAC flying above them at about the same time. When Captain Willoughby regained consciousness at about 1100, he learned about the situation and heard of the valiant efforts of Sergeant First Class Ashley and the other Green Berets to reach the TOC. As soon as he was able, Willoughby was in radio contact with both his team sergeant and his company commander.

At about 1430, Lieutenant Colonel Schungel asked Captain Willoughby if he thought that they could survive the night, as help would be available in the morning. The answer was clear. They had no food, no water, and were almost out of ammunition. All of them had received wounds and were not quite recovered from the explosion that had given them all concussions earlier that morning. There was no way they could last the night. Any determined attack by the NVA would bring a quick death to these Green Berets, but somehow they kept the nosy NVA from further inquiries by ricocheting bullets up the stairwell and through the hole in the TOC wall.

Willoughby gathered his exhausted, battle-worn troops around him after getting the call from Schungel. "We've got two options. One, stay here and go through another night of this and see if they can reinforce us tomorrow, or two, we can make a breakout."

Willoughby recalls, "I didn't really put it to a vote, but I said, 'Give me your thoughts.'"

Paul Longgrear was very clear on what he thought they should do, and it was not to stay the night. As Longgrear remembers the situation,

When Schungel called Willoughby, he told him that the marines were not coming, but if we could hold out till dawn, reinforcements would come. When Willoughby told us, I went ballistic! I said, "You guys can stay here and die like a worm, but I'm going up on top and die like a man, and I'm taking my two men with me." I grabbed Moreland and he grabbed my rifle with both hands. I kept yelling at him, "Moreland! Moreland! It's me, Longgrear! Let go of my rifle!" We were immediately in what was almost a death battle. He had no idea of who I was. His eyes were glazed over. He was looking right through me! We rolled around on the floor. He was my size, and I had a real struggle even when I finally got on top. I had to press my rifle across his neck to keep him down, but he was strong enough to keep me from getting loose. Fragos came over to give me a hand. "What do you want me to do?" he asked.

"Pop him with morphine!" I answered.

"But he's got a bad head wound and it could be fatal!"

"Son, if you've got a better idea, let me know right now! He's got to let go of me!"

Fragos injected the struggling Moreland, whom Longgrear was certain was completely oblivious to reality and dying. Moreland had been in grievous pain and needed relief. Longgrear remembers, "I grabbed Early and started to carry him out the door. The other five talked me into waiting a bit, as they had made up their minds. We called Schungel and said, 'We're coming out!'"

By 1500, the time had come to evacuate the TOC. According to Longgrear, "Schungel said, 'If you're going to break out, let's do it in an orderly fashion.' He gave Willoughby instructions."

The best way out of the TOC was to lay down covering fire by the slow-moving World War–II vintage A-1E Skyraiders. The Spads proved highly effective for close air support due to their slow speed and daring pilots. The single-engine propeller-driven planes dropped 250-pound bombs within thirty to one hundred feet of the TOC. After their bomb racks were empty, they strafed the NVA with their 20mm guns. Although the

Skyraiders suppressed the NVA firing on the hill, occasional grenades still rolled into the TOC. Firing erupted once more on the north and east areas of the camp, and again Willoughby called for close air support against these enemy positions.

Willoughby had agreed with the FAC to make three "for real" bombing runs against the NVA on the hill to keep their heads low. On the next several dry runs, as the planes approached, Willoughby hoped that the NVA would again take cover while he and his men made their escape.

All of the men in the TOC were wounded, and the MIKE Force medic, Specialist Fourth Class Moreland, was obviously dying. Willoughby had to either leave Moreland behind or risk losing more men to save him.

The men from the TOC, minus the dead or dying Moreland, climbed out of their battered bunker and headed for safety. It would be about three hundred meters to the far edge of the camp's outer-perimeter wire, and perhaps another five hundred meters to the old camp. As they emerged from the bunker, Lieutenant Longgrear took the point of the small group, cautiously wending their way to ground level due to the total destruction of the stairs.

For Longgrear, the escape will always be like something that happened yesterday. "I had the point. As soon as I got to ground level, I ducked behind the barrels to cover the others. Brooks dragged Early up the stringers of the knocked-out stairs. Then came Dooms, who was helping Emanuel Phillips get out. It was too crowded to stay behind the barrels, so I hopped over them. I was exposed then. Fragos was helping Willoughby and came out last, as I recall."

Willoughby moved his men out carefully, to minimize exposure to enemy fire. Although Willoughby remembers the exit slightly differently than Longgrear, both recall agreeing that if any of them became wounded, the others would have to keep moving. Willoughby's multiple shrapnel wounds rendered his right arm nearly useless. He remembers having his Green Beret in his pocket.

Longgrear could not believe the sight as he emerged from the TOC. The familiar landmarks no longer existed, wiped out by the shelling and bombs. Only a few destroyed Russian-made tanks were still upright. The plan called for the men to move out in the direction of supply bunker number 2 in the northeastern corner of the camp. Longgrear, still the point man, without landmarks and in a weakened condition, became disoriented momentarily.

Seeing something out of the corner of his eye, he turned quickly to see two NVA armed with a machine gun. They were calmly counting a large stack of money looted from several of his dead MIKE Force troops. Longgrear had paid his men in cash just two days before. Realizing that the NVA machine gun crew could wipe out all seven of the escaping Green Berets, Longgrear fired what he wanted to be a six-round burst. He had loaded an eighteen-round magazine just before leaving the TOC. Four bullets cut down the NVA machine gunners just as his rifle stopped firing and his bad ankle gave way. He went down in a heap, rolled automatically, and thought this was the end for him.

At this moment, Lieutenant Longgrear's outlook on life changed permanently. Everything seemed to stop—the jets in the sky, the noise around him—almost as if the world, or perhaps his destiny, was waiting for him. "God, please don't let me die! I don't want to die, not now. I want to live!" Longgrear remembers praying, recognizing just how mortal he was. A peace came over him like a warm blanket, and suddenly reality returned. The jets were zooming and Longgrear struggled to his feet, using his disabled weapon as a crutch. For some reason the enemy did not fire at him, and he hobbled as quickly as possible to rejoin the TOC survivors, not moving at top speed themselves. The little group had traversed only about seventy-five yards.

True to form, Lieutenant Quy of the Vietnamese Special Forces was waiting for them at the front gate with a jeep. They piled in and Lieutenant Quy sped off to Old Lang Vei and safety. It was 1600.

8

Painful Extraction

On the evening of 6 February, members of the super-secret MACV-SOG were at their camp on the southwestern corner of Khe Sanh. They were not overwhelming in number. The MACV-SOG compound at Khe Sanh was Forward Operating Base Three (FOB-3). The daily routine was hair-raising. They were out of country more than they were in country: Laos and North Vietnam were their operating territories. Usually operating with two or three Green Berets plus an equal or greater number of Bru tribesmen, the recon teams had backup when they had to fight their way out of tight situations.

The next largest team they would call for help would be one of their three recon or "Spike" teams. A Spike team would consist of three U.S. Special Forces, usually led by a staff NCO, and nine Bru. The three Spike teams at FOB-3 on 6 February 1968 bore the names of the home states of their leaders: Oklahoma, Wisconsin, and Pennsylvania.

Because of the tense situation, the next largest rescue team, called variously Hurricane, Havoc, or, more commonly, Hatchet Force, moved into FOB-3 from FOB-1 near Phu Bai and Hue, on the coast. First Lt. Allen "Chips" Fleming commanded the Hatchet Force. In addition there was another lieutenant and four NCOs, all Special Forces–qualified. Their thirty-two indigenous troops were Nungs.

The SOG unit on the evening of 6 February heard the unmistakable chatter of Team A-101's .50-caliber machine guns. The firing continued until almost 0300 on 7 February. They could also see the flares going off over the camp during the attack. It was almost like watching fireworks from a great distance. Then, on the morning of 7 February, while Willoughby and his men were trying to survive until being rescued or until they were able to escape, the two designated Spike teams went on standby. Maj. George Quamo, the special projects officer for the SOG at FOB-3, ordered two Spike teams, Oklahoma and Pennsylvania, as well as Chips Fleming's Hatchet Force, to be ready to go.

It is difficult to tell elite troops that they cannot go on a crucial mission, that they must stay behind in reserve. Such was the case at FOB-3. The term *strap hangers* originally designated eager paratroops who wanted to go along on a mission but had not been assigned. They would have to stand in line behind the designated "stick" or paratroop team and hope that there would be time for them to bail out behind the last man in the stick. The jump-master would make the final decision at the time. One of the strap hangers for the Lang Vei rescue mission was the senior enlisted man at FOB-3. Com. Sgt. Maj. Richard E. Pegram would go in with the Oklahoma team commanded by Sfc. Robert L. Cavanaugh. Even though

Pegram outranked him, Cavanaugh was in charge of the Oklahoma Spike team.

Bob Cavanaugh was a veteran of many over-the-wire missions into Indian Country and foreign countries that were forbidden by the Geneva Accords. Laos and North Vietnam were operating ground to SOG men like Cavanaugh. He had a recon team on Co Roc Mountain in Laos. He took his men into one of the many caves and tunnels that run like rabbit warrens all through the three-thousand-foot-high mountain. Some of the tunnels contained railroad tracks. The tracks enabled the NVA to wheel out their big guns, fire, and pull back far enough to be safe from counterbattery fire from the big guns of the Americans. The cave that Cavanaugh's team entered was vacant except for some interesting equipment, and Cavanaugh had his hands full trying to keep the Bru from playing the NVA cymbals they found.

The Spike teams had trained the Bru well. Probably the smallest of the montagnards, the Bru looked much like Australian Aborigines. They had particular problems learning to throw grenades, due to their size and the unnatural throwing motion. The SOG learned quickly the value of a grenade sump, a safety hole dug in a bunker for a dropped live grenade. The Bru even tried their best to pronounce the names of their American teams, and the SOG unofficially renamed the teams "Oklahome," "Pennsavane," and "Wisacon."

Helicopters dropped Cavanaugh's team at the LZ near Lang Vei on the way back from Co Roc. They had truck transport back to FOB-3. The timing was nearly perfect, except that Cavanaugh, on his third and last tour in Vietnam, was cutting it a little close. The pickup was the day before the Tet Offensive began. Their initial pickup vehicle broke down on Route 9, and Cavanaugh sat on the hood like a sitting duck until a relief truck arrived. Many times the SOG men did not carry weapons around FOB-3. This was not bravado; they had experienced so many narrow escapes that they never got serious about the war until they had left South Vietnam.

MACV-SOG used the village at Lang Vei as a base for training and launching missions on the ground. They had lived there until they moved up to the old French fort. M.Sgt. Charles J. "Skip" Minnicks was the senior enlisted man at FOB-3. Minnicks ran three Spike teams (usually three American Special Forces and six to eight Bru montagnards in each team) until then-Capt. (soon to be Maj.) George Quamo arrived. FOB-3 received about three days' advance notice of Quamo's arrival.

At first the nine Special Forces NCOs were bitter. They surmised that Quamo was either a misfit or something very special as a leader. The enlisted men could not understand why a man who would soon be field grade needed to command nine veterans like themselves. When Quamo arrived, he encountered an icy reception. Skip Minnicks, the former leader, probably took Quamo's assignment hardest of all. He had lost his position as chief honcho of this fine group of fighting men.

Captain Quamo had not been in FOB-3 long before he decided to sit down with his resentful senior NCO and clear the air.

"Look, Skip," Minnicks remembers Quamo saying, "you're fighting me tooth and nail. You know, we've got one mission, and the mission hasn't changed. They sent me up here, I'm in charge, whether you like it or not, and what the hell do you expect me to do? I've got to run the place."

Minnicks realized that the man was right. "It ended up I would have crawled down the barrel of a cannon for him," he says today, "I loved the guy."

The other men also relented. They had been working independently without direct supervision long enough that the presence of an officer had at first seemed to put them and their work under a microscope, but they soon found out that George Quamo was no ordinary officer. He could have remained in the relative safety of FOB-3 and let Minnicks and the others do the over-the-wire recon work, but that was not the way George Quamo worked. Bob Cavanaugh says today that Quamo was the only officer he knew who had the authority to cross the border into Laos, where the unit performed most of its recon work. Cavanaugh also says that every American on Quamo's three Spike teams would have "followed him to hell to put out the fire if he asked."

As THE jeep carrying the TOC survivors reached the old camp shortly after 1600 on 7 February, their dreams of safety exploded with the mortar rounds dropping in front of them. The FAC received a request to again plaster with bombs the Lang Vei camp they had just left. The men at Old Lang Vei had no way of knowing that First Lieutenant Todd remained alive at the new camp, but Todd, searching for hand grenades at the beginning of the battle, had become trapped in the medical bunker and was still there.

Shortly after the TOC survivors arrived at Old Lang Vei, Captain Willoughby was on the radio with the FAC. He recalls the exchange as follows:

"Are you expecting reinforcements?" the FAC asked him.

"No, they turned us down."

"You have an extremely large force en route to your location."

"How large?"

"I would guesstimate a battalion."

"What do you anticipate is their ETA?"

"Thirty to forty minutes."

"I appreciate the information."

"Can I engage these people?"

"What do you have?"

"I have fast movers [jets] on site."

"Friend, be my guest. They don't belong to me."

Willoughby never saw this engagement between American air power and the NVA infantry who were on a forced march from near Khe Sanh village to the Old Lang Vei camp, but the FAC's ETA sounded accurate to him. Without interference from American fast movers, the oncoming NVA would pose a serious threat to the surviving Green Berets at the Old Lang Vei camp.

While the aircraft did as requested, Lieutenant Colonel Schungel called for helicopters to remove the survivors to safety. Responses to his medevac requests were less prompt than the requests for bombs. While the Green Berets waited, they rendered the best medical care they could for the wounded. Rich Allen remembers thinking of Custer's last stand as he bandaged seemingly countless wounded men. Soon American warbirds filled the air. From the latest model jet fighter-bombers to the Douglas Skyraiders of World War II vintage, aircraft provided protection for the marine CH-46 Sea Knight helicopters. Helicopter gunships also swung into action. The brave defenders of Lang Vei, at least the Americans, were coming out— most of them.

COL. DAVID Lownds, commander of the Khe Sanh combat base and of the 26th Marine Regiment, today says that although the rescue mission had been in place for some months, the decision not to go in was based on tactical considerations.

I knew that at some point that place [Lang Vei] was going to come under attack. So I took a battalion and ran them down there, not on the road, because I realized that when the time came, I probably couldn't go down the road. And it took the battalion, 1/26 [First Battalion, 26th Marine Regiment], under [Lt. Col.] Jim Wilkinson, moving as fast as they could, not going down the road, as I remember, roughly twelve hours. So that ruled out that possibility. The second possibility was to go down the road. The next possibility probably was to go by helicopter. Landing zones

there were covered by tanks—tanks on my landing zone. So I couldn't go in by helicopter. Going
down the road, where the tanks were, they would
have pretty well controlled that road and so I really had no possibility of getting those people
out, when he [Willoughby] had nothing to fight
with.

In other words, he just had his army people,
and so there was nothing I could do but try to get
the air wing to see if they were willing to go in.
My helicopters were not suitable for that mission.
As I remember it, the army wouldn't send anybody in. And as I remember it, finally the Marine
Corps sent in some Hueys, which was probably
correct and the only thing that could have gotten
in there to get them.

Authors John Prados and Ray Stubbe, in *Valley of
Decision*, tell about Wilkinson sending Alpha Company of the First Battalion, 26th Marines, on the practice run. In their book, Capt. John W. Raymond
commanded Alpha Company, which went through the
bush, avoided both roads and trails, and accomplished
the feat in nineteen hours. Wilkinson today remembers
the practice run exactly as Prado and Stubbe described
it. Lownds, however, is certain that it was a battalion he
sent that November day in 1967. As he tells it:

They got partway down, and I took a helicopter. I
wanted to go in and talk to Jim about what kind of
progress he was making, but I got halfway down
there and the helicopter pilot told [the troops on

the ground]: "Pop a smoke so we can find you."

So they popped a red smoke and we went down and all of a sudden we were sitting down in an outfit of North Vietnamese. I hollered, "Get up there!" We would have been shot down.

I knew that they couldn't get there through the underbrush, and there was no sense going down the road with tanks on there, or landing the helicopters with tanks on the landing zone.

Another thing was, Willoughby wanted artillery support. I told him I'd give him all the artillery support I could, just tell me where he wanted it. So we gave it to him. Then finally he said, "How about air bursts?" I said if that's what you want, we'll do it. So we did. Then he said, "Well, they're still coming."

And he said . . . he was going to ask the army to send helicopters in. He tried, but the army wouldn't help him.

Asked if it was he who had made the initial decision not to send in the relief force, Colonel Lownds answered, "I think Tompkins asked me, 'Can you get in there?' I can't get in there, I told him. I can't get down the road, I can't go off the road, I can't fly helicopters in there."

"Our mission was really to support them with artillery fire, which we did, which we practiced, and fired. I couldn't see risking one thousand marines because, honestly, if I thought there was a chance they could get there I would have tried it, but I don't think there was."

· · ·

THE MARINES' decision not to send in a relief force was not the final curtain call for the brave defenders at Lang Vei. Their fate rested ultimately much further up the chain of command.

Col. Jonathan Ladd, as commander of the 5th Special Forces Group (Airborne), was Lieutenant Colonel Schungel's immediate superior. Ladd called Saigon twice during the early morning hours to awaken his own immediate superior, Gen. William C. Westmoreland, the Military Assistance Command Vietnam commander (ComUSMACV).

His aide awakened Westmoreland the first time after the marines at Khe Sanh heard Joel Johnson's radio call from Old Lang Vei, reporting that two tanks were sitting on the most likely helicopter landing zone, a cleared supply-drop area. The tanks' presence ruled out any vertical assault (helicopter landing), and Colonel Lownds had told Captain Willoughby that the marines would not send in a rescue force. In Da Nang, Ladd had placed his first call to General Westmoreland.

Westmoreland was the immediate superior of the 3d Marine Amphibious Force (III MAF) commanding general, Lt. Gen. Robert E. Cushman, Jr. Cushman was the immediate superior of Maj. Gen. Rathvon Tompkins, the commanding general of the 3d Marine Division. Tompkins was the immediate superior of Col. David Lownds, who commanded the 26th Regiment of marines at Khe Sanh combat base. Westmoreland reported to Adm. U.S. Grant "Oley" Sharp, U.S. Navy, the commander in chief, Pacific, whose headquarters were in Hawaii. Whether or not the chain of command had any bearing on Westmoreland's responses to the relief missions proposed is unknown.

Westmoreland told Ladd that the relief remained the responsibility of Cushman and Tompkins in I Corps. In essence he was saying that he could not, from hundreds of air miles away, overrule the commander on the scene. It was at that time, approximately 0150, that Westmoreland authorized the marine artillery to use COFRAM.

Colonel Ladd had enough volunteers from the 5th Special Forces Group (Airborne) to attempt a rescue, if one was possible. The men of the elite scout unit of Project DELTA had volunteered en masse to jump into Lang Vei. Paul Longgrear's immediate superior, MIKE Force battalion commander Maj. Adam Husar, was also raising a force to go to embattled Lang Vei.

At 0400 Maj. LeRoy Edwards, Company C operations officer, called Col. Franklin L. Smith at 3d Marine Amphibious Force. Edwards asked Smith to send in the marine relief force at first light. Five minutes later, General Cushman and General Tompkins talked over the request. At 0406 Company C received a negative reply. An angry Colonel Ladd called General Westmoreland for the second time, told the ComUSMACV of the second turndown, and asked permission from the former paratrooper to mount his own relief operation.

Brig. Gen. John Chaisson, U.S. Marine Corps, was General Westmoreland's Combat Operations Center director. When Colonel Ladd's urgent calls for General Westmoreland came in, it was Chaisson who had to awaken the ComUSMACV. In his autobiography, *A Soldier Reports*, Westmoreland says that he replied that he would not intervene in the Lang Vei situation until he could ascertain more facts. He says that just after dawn broke on 7 February, he called his I Corps Army and Marine Corps commanders together for a meeting in Da Nang, where he flew to meet with them. "Of first priority," writes Westmoreland, "was the crisis at Lang Vei. I directed General Cushman to provide helicopters for a relief force of CIDG troops with Special Forces advisers to bring out American and South Vietnamese survivors."

Westmoreland's account then says that of the fourteen Americans who got out of Lang Vei, all but three had wounds, and that the ten missing Americans were listed as killed in action. As in many other records of the battle, Westmoreland's casualty count is inaccurate. Only one Green Beret extracted from Old Lang Vei was not wounded. The previous inaccuracies have probably been due to the fact that S.Sgt. Emanuel Phillips and Sp4c. Franklin Dooms suffered internal bleeding as the result of severe concussion wounds. Captain Willoughby believes that one or both of them bled from the ears. If so, the blood would have mixed with the dirt, smoke, and explosive residue on their exposed body parts, making wound identification difficult. Both Dooms and Phillips received Purple Hearts.

In addition, ten of the twenty-four did not die, as General Westmoreland relates: in 1973, S.Sgt. Dennis L. Thompson, Sfc. Harvey G. Brande, and Sp4c. William G. McMurry returned to the States with the other American prisoners of war. Two of the ten, Sfc. Eugene Ashley, Jr., and Sfc. Earl F. Burke, were later confirmed as killed in action. During the extraction, the relief force inadvertently missed bringing out Ashley's remains. Contained in a body bag, they rested in the jeep in which Ashley had died until found by the First Air Cavalry during April 1968. The Cavalry also found Burke's remains, buried in a shallow grave just off Route 9. Army officials listed the five others as missing in action. Strong evidence suggests that Sp4c. James L. Moreland and Sfc. Charles W. Lindewald died at Lang Vei, where Sfc. Kenneth Hanna may also have died. Sfc. James W. Holt and Sp5c. Daniel R. Phillips are the real mysteries.

COL. JONATHAN F. Ladd, former commanding officer of the Special Forces in Vietnam, said in a 1977 interview (part of the General Abrams oral-history project) that he had to go to Abrams about the relief of Lang Vei.

Colonel Ladd says that he visited Lang Vei camp the night before the battle but left to get some antitank mines and more LAWs, and that he could hear the tanks moving around but did not see them until the morning of 7 February. No other participants in the battle who were interviewed for this book recalled Colonel Ladd visiting Lang Vei, nor did anyone else record hearing the tanks the night before.

Ladd states that he flew to Da Nang to visit the 3d Marine Amphibious Force Commander, Lieutenant General Cushman. Cushman was prepared to give

Ladd the antitank mines but was overruled by the MACV staff in Saigon, says Ladd. "The people down in Saigon wouldn't believe that there were tanks up there," thus Ladd had no need for antitank mines. Ladd further relates that they would not give the mines to the Special Forces. Ladd did not know why, but generally the mines were not used in camps where there were indigenous personnel. However, this was a fighting camp that included no dependents.

When told he could not have the antitank mines, Ladd became "furious," especially after he had talked the marines into giving them to him. The mines could have made a big difference in the outcome of the battle.

When Colonel Ladd flew over Lang Vei on the morning of 7 February, he says he saw "three tanks up on top of the thing"—presumably the TOC, because he goes on to say, "we'd run our aerials underground so they were still in communication, but everybody was down underneath in the underground camp because there were tanks on top." As Captain Willoughby recalls, after the NVA had blown the hole in the wall, the men in the TOC had inserted a radio antenna in the opening. He remembers no underground communication equipment other than communication wire between the various defensive positions in the camp.

Ladd says that during his flight over the scarred battleground, "I didn't see any infantry." While he was talking to the camp on the radio, he heard someone say, "We don't think there is much infantry. There isn't much, but there are some around the edges." It is not clear to whom he was speaking at this time, but it was probably someone in the TOC, perhaps relaying through Old Lang Vei and the FAC. Ladd says he then went back to Khe Sanh and asked if Colonel Lownds would execute the contingency plan and rescue the Lang Vei survivors, because he still had three hundred people there.

After the Khe Sanh marine commander replied that it would be a suicide mission, Ladd says, he reiterated that he had just flown over Lang Vei and felt certain that the contingency plan did not have to be a suicide mission. Ladd says he then left Khe Sanh and flew to Da Nang to meet with General Westmoreland, who had flown there from Saigon regarding a marine civic-action meeting. Westmoreland had given Ladd a moment of his time, with no positive results for the Special Forces commander.

A frustrated Ladd now tried another approach. He telephoned General Abrams and briefed him on the events that were taking place at the Lang Vei Special Forces camp. Ladd says he told General Abrams that he was not getting any action from General Westmoreland, after which Abrams called General Norman Anderson, commanding the 1st Marine Air Wing.

Anderson was the man who would have to supply the CH-46 helicopters that would fly in the relief force and fly out the survivors and their covering force. According to Ladd's account, Abrams told Anderson that he was ordering Ladd to proceed at the earliest possible opportunity with the evacuation of Lang Vei, and Anderson was to provide the necessary aircraft. "So Anderson was a great help; they dropped those CBUs all over the top of the camp."

Gen. William C. Westmoreland says it was definitely he who made the decision to send in the marine helicopters. He also says that General Abrams, as commander of MACV Forward (a branch of Westmoreland's own headquarters established at Phu Bai in early February), would have had the authority to make such a decision. Abrams was his personal representative in the I Corps area.

Westmoreland's autobiography makes clear that Lieutenant General Cushman, as commander of the 3d Marine Amphibious Force, did an effective job in commanding his marines. However, Cushman was reluctant to make decisions regarding the increasing numbers of army troops in I Corps, previously regarded as Marine Corps territory. The situation had developed to the point that Westmoreland was becoming nervous about it, with I Corps bordering North Vietnam. It was not just the presence of two NVA divisions near Khe Sanh. There was also one NVA division in the DMZ north of the Rockpile, in close proximity to Khe Sanh, as well as a division near Da Nang, and a reinforced division at Hue. Information indicated two more NVA divisions in or south of the DMZ near the coast, making a total known presence of seven NVA divisions in that northern area.

General Westmoreland had been planning to establish a U.S. Army Corps headquarters in the northern provinces that, under the command of the 3d Marine Amphibious Force, would exercise control over army units in the area. The establishment of a temporary branch of his own headquarters, which became MACV Forward under Gen. Creighton Abrams, was necessary because of the rapid buildup of army forces in the north. The establishment and coordination of the Army Corps headquarters would require more time. Westmoreland credits his chief of staff, Maj. Gen. Walter T. "Dutch" Kerwin, with the concept of an interim solution.

When General Westmoreland asked Abrams to assume command of MACV Forward, he placed him in control of all American ground forces. These included, he says in *A Soldier Reports*, "Army, Marine Corps, and shore-based contingents of the U.S. Navy—in the two provinces north of the Hai Van Pass." Abrams would work in close association with 3d Marine Amphibious Force headquarters. Westmoreland realized that the position in which he was placing Abrams meant that "quick decisions would have to be made in [his] name."

Westmoreland clearly had complete faith in Creighton Abrams, the man who would eventually replace him as ComUSMACV. Abrams had much combat experience, commencing in World War II, and was a solid commander who would make the right decisions. He demonstrated his expertise in commanding various combat arms in the liberation of Hue, captured by the communists during the Tet Offensive.

In his autobiography, Westmoreland does not give an exact date for the establishment of the MACV Forward headquarters, stating only that it was in early February 1968. It is certainly possible that Abrams could have made the decision and Westmoreland confirmed it. It is also possible to reconcile Colonel Ladd's and General Westmoreland's recollections of who gave the order to use marine helicopters in the extraction: If Gen. Norman Anderson received General Abrams's order, as Colonel Ladd recalls, this could have been because Abrams had the authority from Westmoreland to do so. Westmoreland says in his book that he gave Cushman a direct order, in their meeting on 7 February, to give Baldwin the helicopters.

In any case, either Westmoreland or Abrams (or perhaps both of them) gave the order to fly the marine choppers into Old Lang Vei.

LT. COL. DANIEL L. Baldwin, III, the senior MACV-SOG commander in the north, volunteered his FOB-3 troops to perform the rescue mission. Following the decision by Westmoreland and his commanders to accept Baldwin's plan, Baldwin took off from Da Nang in an ARVN H-34 chopper. He headed for FOB-3 at Khe Sanh to set the plan in action. Unfortunately, Baldwin's chopper never completed its mission. The vintage chopper lost power before it reached its destination and made a forced landing. Although the crew made temporary repairs and got the bird back in the air, they refused to fly anywhere but back to the barn, in this case Phu Bai. Consequently, Lieutenant Colonel Baldwin had to settle for a single-sideband radio communication of his planned relief mission to Maj. George Quamo at FOB-3.

Quamo carried out Baldwin's plan, going first to the man who would be the NCO in charge of the mission, M.Sgt. Skip Minnicks. According to Minnicks, Quamo "didn't pull any punches at all. 'Look, it's a suicide mission. I don't think we're coming back, but I can't leave those fellows over there. I'm going over there and try. I'd like you to ask for volunteers,' " Minnicks says he asked his veteran staff NCO.

Master Sergeant Minnicks did as his boss requested. There was no problem getting volunteers from an elite group of soldiers like MACV-SOG. Nearly everyone volunteered, even after being told that it could be a suicide mission. S.Sgt. Charles Berg had only seven days left to serve. He was, in the opinion of his peers, an excellent combat soldier. His MACV-SOG friends were trying to talk him into reenlisting, which would have meant an automatic promotion to sergeant first class. Berg had just completed three years in country and was ready for the tranquillity of the real world again. His good friend Bob Cavanaugh teased him that morning about coming along, but Berg replied good-naturedly, "You guys are going to get your asses shot off! I'm staying here this time."

Later that day, 7 February 1968, Charles Berg was carrying an armload of supplies out of the medical bunker, anticipating the return of his friends from Quamo's "suicide mission." Just as he stepped outside, shrapnel from an artillery round, which he believes was a 152mm, took his leg off at the hip. Berg owes his life to the quick response of medic Robert Scully.

The FOB-3 Command sergeant major, Richard E. Pegram, had volunteered to take Berg's place. M.Sgt. Minnicks would lead the point unit. The point unit landed first and provided protection for the landing zone, until Quamo's larger main force arrived on the ground and quickly dispersed to cover the whole perimeter. Minnicks had not been happy to learn that Pegram was going along.

Minnicks had confronted the senior enlisted man, whose job at the time was more of an administrative and planning nature than operational. Pegram was an outstanding combat soldier, but Minnicks did not want him on this mission. "Because of your rank," Minnick recalls saying, "you will take my place, and you cannot. You don't know our hand and arm signals, you don't know our commands."

"Don't be crazy," Minnicks says Pegram promptly came back. "I'm going in there as a grunt. I'm going in there as a private. I'm going to carry a rifle. You're going to tell me what to do."

"He was a hell of a fellow," Minnicks says today of the command sergeant major, who made it through this mission but not a later one. It was certainly not conventional for a command sergeant major to be willing to act as a private in order to go along on what might be a suicide mission.

Reports of the number of Americans and indigenous troops coming in to Old Lang Vei vary. Skip Minnicks thinks that perhaps half of the forty-plus force was U.S. Special Forces from MACV-SOG. First Lt. Chips Fleming of the Hatchet Force recalls having in his group four other Americans besides himself and about thirty-two Nungs.

Official records show the relief force earning fourteen awards for valor, plus four Purple Hearts to other Special Forces soldiers. Authors Prados and Stubbe list ten Americans and forty indigenous (strikers) as the relief force. Judging from the medals count alone, Minnicks's estimate may be closest to the actual number of American troops involved.

The Marine Corps CH-46 Sea Knights assembled at FOB-3 at 1500. While Major Quamo briefed the pilots, the relief force piled on to the marine choppers, prepared for the mission. Sfc. Bob Cavanaugh commanded the Oklahoma team that included Sgt. Maj. (acting Pvt.) Richard Pegram and Sp5c. William M. Harris. Cavanaugh was very nervous as they sat on the FOB-3 helo pad. He knew that any second this prime target would be receiving NVA incoming 152mm mail. Liftoff time was 1630.

Major Quamo was in radio contact with Lieutenant Colonel Schungel at Old Lang Vei. Earlier Schungel had also reestablished radio contact with the TOC. He knew that his men there were in a precarious situation: their very existence had nearly reached its end. They were ready to fight to the death in their underground hell, and Sergeant First Class Ashley had given his life in five unsuccessful attempts to try to rescue his fellow Green Berets in the TOC.

The Green Berets on the ground waited in great anxiety as they saw the marine CH-46 Sea Knight relief choppers circling over their position at the Old Lang Vei camp. Miles Wilkins remembers that the marine choppers were

Way up in the air, and they wanted us to mark with smoke. Of course, there were those big guns over there [Co Roc Mountain in Laos], and the guys were afraid they were just going to mark themselves as a target. They marked them, but they still weren't coming down. Then some of the Huey jockeys came in. They were trying to load our people on, and the Laotians were trying to get on. The Laotians were literally pulling them [the choppers] out of the air. One of the guys [Long-grear] was just throwing the Laotians off and then just standing up in the door with his weapon as though he was going to spray them. Then they backed off.

Paul Longgrear remembers that anxiety and wondering whether the marine pilots would determine that they could not risk the precious choppers to land in such a hostile environment. The circling flight pattern shows that they must have been at least apprehensive. Longgrear says that one army helo dropped out of the circling flight "like they were giving corporate birth to it. Without circling, it drops straight for the helo marker on the pad. It was flown by army pilots."

It was about 1715 when the first relief chopper descended through a hail of small arms and mortars. Some accounts indicate that the first chopper to land carried the commander of the rescue team, Maj. George Quamo. Paul Longgrear, who was the first one to jump on the slick when it landed, insists that there were no non-aviators on the helicopter except the door gunner/crew chief. Whatever the case, the overloaded UH-1D chopper took out the three Green Berets who could not walk, along with the oft-wounded Lieutenant Colonel Schungel and a number of others. Next came the marine CH-46 choppers, carrying in the MACV-SOG Spike teams and Hatchet Force, who would set up a temporary defensive perimeter to protect the evacuation.

Lieutenant Colonel Baldwin, now stranded in Phu Bai, planned the "exfiltration," perhaps a more accurate term than *evacuation* or *extraction*. Major Quamo fine-tuned and coordinated his plan.

With Quamo in one of those circling choppers was Sgt. Richard D. Mullowney, Jr., of the SOG unit, who would that day perform in such a manner as to be awarded a Silver Star. He recalls not at all liking the circling routine. They were at low altitude, were not even flying at four or five thousand feet, says Mullowney, who after the war became a civilian pilot. At that height, ground fire could have brought down the whole rescue mission.

Lieutenant Longgrear, badly wounded himself, somehow managed to clear the Laotian troops that swamped the first chopper so that it could evacuate the most seriously wounded Green Berets. Longgrear was able to bluff most of the Laotians off the chopper as he entered the starboard side. His disabled CAR-15 rifle served one last purpose without firing a shot: when he worked the bolt, the Laotian contingency did not call his bluff. Longgrear put on his most menacing look, and the soldiers of the Elephant Battalion did not challenge him.

Some of them had twisted and bound their hands into the netting that forms the seats in the Huey, and Longgrear had to use the butt end of the weapon to forcibly remove them. He then stood guard on the port side of the chopper as the other Green Berets entered the starboard side. The chopper became so crowded that Longgrear remembers Lieutenant Colonel Schungel being draped across other bodies on the floor of the chopper. Without an actual head count, Longgrear believes that there were about a dozen or possibly more on board as the chopper roared away to Khe Sanh and the relative safety of the combat base, where the now-repaired runway had C-130s ready to evacuate the seriously wounded.

The second chopper landed the MACV-SOG Green Berets. They secured the LZ so that the other choppers could land with the main body of the relief force, including the Brus of the recon teams and the Nungs of the Hatchet Force.

Sgt. Stephen Kirk led his squad of indigenous mercenaries off the helicopter, under intense enemy mortar and automatic-weapons fire, to the southwest section of the Old Lang Vei camp. With a well-executed squad maneuver, Kirk was able to gain fire superiority over the enemy, disrupt their advance, and compel them to withdraw under fire.

As the wounded and exhausted leader of A-101 was about to board his evacuation chopper, he turned and saluted in the direction of the overrun camp he had commanded from its inception. Captain Willoughby remembers looking at it through tears, saying, "Lang Vei camp belongs to God and the dead."

Sgt. Richard Allen, the only unwounded member of the original twenty-four Green Berets to make it to Old Lang Vei, was making certain that the Green Berets got on the relief choppers first. He soon had indigenous personnel beating on him to let them on the choppers ahead of the combat soldiers. More than one of the Laotians, some of whom had thrown away their weapons to expedite getting on the choppers, received a broken jaw that let them know a determined Allen would do his assigned duty, enforcing the pecking order for evacuation.

After making five charges at the new camp, carrying the mortally wounded Ashley back down the hill, helping patch up countless wounded, and loading them onto the choppers, Allen had had it. Events had taken their toll despite his superb physical condition, and Allen collapsed to his knees some ten meters from the helicopter that could whisk him away to safety.

One of the helicopter crew beckoned to him, yelling to "get his butt in gear and get on." There was no one left to help Allen, and he was too exhausted to save himself. He could not move. All of a sudden, just to the right of his right knee, a burst from an AK-47 assault rifle kicked up the dirt. "Somewhere I had that last ounce of energy," Allen says. "I jumped to my feet and ran as fast as I could and just dove into the helicopter." Thus the only unwounded survivor of the battle escaped intact.

The choppers, once loaded, returned to Khe Sanh. The marine CH-46s made only the initial trip to bring out the survivors and did not return to Old Lang Vei. Army UH-1D helicopters completed the extraction mission. The rescue force, according to Sgt. Richard Mullowney, had initially planned to move out to the south on foot. The only problem was that some very unfriendly NVA troops populated the hill they were going to cross.

Expressing their displeasure with the planned move, they sent rocket, mortar, and small-arms fire in the direction of the rescue force. Mullowney, Sergeant Major Pegram, and Sfc. Gilbert Secor all used 3.5-inch rocket launchers against the enemy positions on the hill to the south. They finally suppressed the NVA fire by firing longer and more accurately.

Sfc. Bob Cavanaugh remembers M.Sgt. Skip Minnicks and his team clearing the LZ with deadly fire prior to the return of the army choppers to extract the extraction force. When the choppers returned, Minnicks recalls his talk with the first pilot who landed. Before his rapid descent to the LZ, the pilot asked Minnicks, "Is the landing zone clear?"

"Sure," came the answer from Minnicks, who now says that he would have told the chopper pilot the LZ was clear even if the enemy was standing on it. The extraction force needed the choppers immediately, if not sooner. The pilot later told Minnicks, "I knew your idea of a clear LZ and mine were different when the first round went through my windshield!"

The last of the four Marine CH-46 helicopters carried out the more seriously wounded indigenous troops. Also carried out were key Vietnamese officers, senior NCOs, and interpreters. Due to a premium on helicopter space, many CIDG and MIKE Force indigenous personnel, as well as nearly all the Laotians, were left behind at Old Lang Vei. Many CIDG simply faded into the surrounding areas. Surprisingly, Major Husar later wrote to Lieutenant Longgrear (hospitalized in Japan) that more than 120 of his MIKE Force successfully returned to friendly hands via various methods. More than 100 CIDG also found their way back to safety. It was 11 February before Colonel Soulang and approximately 100 of his troops were flown from Khe Sanh to Da Nang. On 15 February they returned to Savannakhet.

• • •

JUST AFTER 1700, Lieutenant Todd left the medical bunker and ran to the destroyed TOC, hoping to find someone else alive. As he entered, he saw the body of Moreland buried in the debris. He quickly exited the TOC and saw a helicopter taking off from Old Lang Vei. He knew he had to get there as fast as he could. Todd received fire until he reached the far side of the hill and was out of sight of the shooters. His fellow Lang Vei Green Beret survivors had already taken off, but the perimeter guards were still there, and he left with them minutes later.

PLANNERS IMMEDIATELY went to work, preparing to go back into the two Lang Vei camps as soon as practicable, under the code name Operation San Francisco. The objective of the proposed mission was the retrieval of the bodies of both U.S. and Vietnamese Special Forces and the burial of the indigenous corpses, but this was not to be. Marine Lt. Gen. Robert Cushman ruled out the mission, saying that the possible military consequences outweighed the humanitarian aspects.

9

Monday Morning Quarterbacking

One of the important happenings in the military, regardless of whether an event occurs in peacetime or in war, is the critique of the event. In peacetime it may be the replay and analysis of a field problem, such as an attack on a fortified position. Participants, planners, and observers first discuss the original mission, then perhaps the planning and execution of the assault phase. The point of the critique is simply to evaluate planning and performance. In wartime, an after-action report replaces the peacetime critique. This may be just the report filed by the commanding officer or whoever was in charge of the friendly forces in an engagement.

In the case of the Battle of Lang Vei, official reports initially listed ten of the twenty-four Green Berets present at the battle as missing in action. In such a case the Department of the Army wants to collect all the information possible to establish the probable fate of those missing men. Consequently, a number of the surviving Green Berets from Lang Vei gave statements (after-action reports) at Company C headquarters in Da Nang on 15 February 1968. The following participants gave official statements: Lt. Col. Daniel F. Schungel, Capt. Frank C. Willoughby, 1st Lt. Thomas E. Todd, S.Sgt. Peter Tiroch, S.Sgt. Emanuel E. Phillips, Sgt. Nickolas Fragos, Sgt. Richard H. Allen, Sp4c. Joel Johnson, and Sp4c. Franklin H. Dooms.

Additionally, army officials debriefed a number of indigenous troops and filed a summary report on 17 February 1968. Because there were eight American fighting men missing in action after the battle, a Board of Inquiry for Missing Persons convened under army regulations AR 15-6 and 600-10, and under U.S. Army, Vietnam regulation 600-1. The board members consisted of three officers: Capt. James A. Goldstine, 1st Lt. Eugene E. Makowski, and 2d Lt. David C. Ehresman. The appointed recorder was the junior officer, 2d Lt. Ehresman. This board, all officers of Company C, determined all the facts about the status of the individuals assigned or attached to Company C who had been classified as missing in action. The board had to convene within ten days after the MIA classification. Headquarters, 5th Special Forces Group (Airborne), had to receive the required five copies of the completed report within fifteen days after the convening date.

The order convening the board listed ten men in Exhibit B as missing in action, but that number included Sergeant First Class Ashley and Sergeant First Class Burke, later confirmed as killed in action. It also included Sergeant First Class Brande, Specialist Fourth Class Moreland, Sergeant First Class Hanna, Sergeant First Class Holt, Sergeant First Class Lindewald, Staff Sergeant Thompson, Sp5c. Daniel Phillips, and Specialist Fourth Class McMurry.

The Board of Inquiry convened at 0800 on 23 February 1968, at Company C headquarters in Da Nang. They began by reading the names of the ten men considered missing in action. Next they read the after-action reports of Lieutenant Colonel Schungel, Captain Willoughby, First Lieutenant Todd, Staff Sergeant Tiroch, S.Sgt. Emanuel Phillips, Sergeant Fragos, Sergeant Allen, Specialist Fourth Class Johnson, and Specialist Fourth Class Dooms. The board also interviewed a member of the security group that had protected the evacuation, Sfc. Gilbert A. Secor.

The board then read the debriefing report of the indigenous personnel. They requested and subsequently interviewed several native troops who had made comments that the board considered pertinent. These were Le Van Quoc, a combat interpreter; Dinh Chep, a platoon leader; and Dinh Dui, a platoon sergeant. All had been with the MIKE Force.

Next the board called the Green Beret survivors who had made statements on 15 February. Second Lieutenant Ehresman swore them in and took their statements. The form used, DA Form 19-24, is the same used in any formal investigation, including for wrongdoing. Because the investigation was noncriminal, the board had the item *accused/suspected* deleted.

Because of the official nature of the investigation, all those interviewed had their rights read under the governing laws of conduct for the military. Specifically, the rights included those outlined in Article 31 of the Uniform Code of Military Justice. The article is straightforward enough, and military justice requires that it be read to each concerned individual.

Each had to signify that he understood he did not have to make any statement whatsoever. If he chose to make a statement, he received instructions that the use of the statement as evidence against him was lawful. Since there was obviously no evidence of wrongdoing, all made their statements to the board.

The Board of Inquiry issued the following conclusions in its report to the commanding officer of the 5th Special Forces Group (Airborne):

(a) SFC Eugene Ashley was killed by a wound received on 7 Feb 68.

(b) SP-4 James W. Moreland was dead or dying when seen by LT Todd at 1700 hours, 7 Feb 68. If alive he would not have survived the night without expert medical treatment.

(c) SP-4 William G. McMurry was seriously injured.

(d) SFC Charles W. Lindewald was seriously injured.

(e) SFC Harvey G. Brande was wounded, probably very seriously.

(f) All others were physically capable of resisting, but may have been captured.

The board also recommended the change of status of Sfc. Eugene Ashley and Sp4c. James W. Moreland from missing in action to killed by hostile action. Finally, it recommended the continuance of the status of all others as missing in action until it received affidavits of those wounded and evacuated from the Republic of Vietnam.

The Battle of Lang Vei was especially significant in

that it was the first time the NVA used armor in an attack. That fact alone is noteworthy enough to generate substantial interest in the battle, from a perspective of possibly changing training methods to include combat against an enemy using tanks in the assault.

The shock effect of an unexpected armor attack can be devastating to troops in the defense, especially those totally unprepared for such an event. It is to the everlasting credit of the CIDG and MIKE Forces, as well as their Green Beret instructors and leaders, that these indigenous forces bravely stood their ground against an armored force. A number of them died in their designated defensive positions while trying to fight against tanks with only small arms, machine guns, grenades, and often ineffective LAWs. No breakdown was listed between the indigenous KIA (killed in action) and MIA, but the total was 209, with another 64 wounded in action.

Had the NVA chosen to use the PT-76 tanks against the marine combat base at Khe Sanh, they would have been sending boys to do a man's job. The marines had six more heavily armored tanks, with larger main guns and probably more experienced crews. They also had ten of the most unsightly vehicles ever to travel on tracks. Named the Ontos, these tank killers sported six 106mm recoilless rifles. The life expectancy of the PT-76s would revert to seconds against that kind of firepower. Lang Vei made much more sense as a target for these light-skinned amphibious tanks, designed for a reconnaissance role rather than as a spearhead for an infantry attack against a well-fortified position.

The NVA had done their homework before attacking

Lang Vei. They knew from their vast intelligence network that U.S. Special Forces could not employ antitank mines in their barbed-wire entanglements because they had indigenous personnel inside the compound. They had even double-checked the accuracy of their information by sending sappers to drive a number of water buffalo into the wire. The Green Berets killed the sappers and dined on buffalo meat, but the NVA learned that the buffalo did not set off any antitank mines in the process. Their information was correct.

Lang Vei was the early warning for the northwest section of I Corps. It sat astride Route 9, and if the NVA wanted to move large numbers of troops against Khe Sanh, they had to remove Lang Vei. The NVA chose units of 304th Division, a veteran group who had fought at Dien Bien Phu. The number of infantry the NVA employed in the assault is unknown, but it must certainly have been in the hundreds.

A total of eleven tanks attacked Lang Vei. The main thrust came from the south, from the trail that leads to Lang Troai. They were the first tanks reported. The first two tanks were almost contemptuous of the defenders, sending sappers out in clear view to cut the wire entanglements. The tank commanders of the two tanks had their hatches open and were exposed to small-arms fire. The first tank had used its searchlight to survey the area at close range before crumpling the wire under its tracks.

This bold action momentarily froze the defenders of 104 Company, but they recovered in time to cut down the sappers and force the tankers to button up their hatches. Some analysts would observe that all the tanks should have overwhelmed one side of the camp, penetrated in force, and then spread out from the camp's center to attack the other companies from the rear.

The massing of the enemy armor could have provided an even more pronounced shock effect for the defenders, but that would have also posed a better target for American air and artillery support. If the NVA had known that American planes would be grounded and spotters unable to accurately place artillery strikes, they could have used such a mass attack. It was obvious, therefore, that they had completed their plans just days prior to the actual attack: no one could have predicted the weather conditions far in advance with any great accuracy.

By attacking from three directions, the NVA undoubtedly caused much more confusion in the ranks of the defenders. The MIKE Force platoon was manning the OP, located between the camp and the Laotian border. The defenders expected any attack to come from this direction, given the arrival some days earlier of the routed Royal Elephant Battalion from their Laotian base. The four tanks that attacked the camp from the west along Route 9 came past the OP, while the infantry, with the help of at least one of the four tanks, overwhelmed it. An OP does not have the defensive capability that the main camp does, intended mostly as an early warning device for the primary defense system.

The remaining two tanks came from the east, from the general direction of Khe Sanh and Old Lang Vei. They served notice to the defenders that the attack was not just a roll-up of their camp by an overwhelming mass frontal attack. That sort of attack would attempt to sweep over them like a tidal wave. It would gain momentum as it headed down Route 9 toward Khe Sanh, perhaps engulfing Old Lang Vei and the Royal Elephant Battalion along the way. Lang Vei was a thorn in the side of the NVA, and perhaps an object lesson for other isolated Special Forces camps. In any case, at this particular time it was the NVA's sole objective in the area from Khe Sanh to the Laotian border.

One cannot analyze the Battle of Lang Vei alone; it must be included in the general context of the siege of Khe Sanh. Whether or not General Westmoreland achieved his objective of using a reinforced marine regiment of some six thousand men at Khe Sanh and its surrounding hilltops to tie up at least two or perhaps three NVA infantry divisions remains speculative even today. Some experts maintain that some of those troops Westmoreland claimed to have tied up at Khe Sanh became heavily involved in the battle for the ancient city of Hue. General Vo Nguyen Giap has claimed that he never had any intention of taking the marine combat base at Khe Sanh and never made more than token ground attacks against it. Some intercepted NVA radio traffic indicates otherwise.

The fact remains that the twenty-four Green Berets at Lang Vei and their MIKE Force and CIDG put up a terrific fight, one that may have shown General Giap just what he could anticipate in any attempt to take Khe Sanh by storm.

Had Lang Vei not existed, there would have been no significant deterrent to NVA movement of a sizable force between the Laotian border and the Khe Sanh base. The use of heavier armor would then have been possible, and vehicle resupply would have been available, although subject to air and artillery attack by the Americans. As General Giap analyzed the tenacious defense by two dozen brave and determined elite American fighting men and a few hundred indigenous troops, he had to realize that an attack on Khe Sanh could indeed prove perilous. Giap would have had to sacrifice many thousands of his best-trained soldiers if he wanted to overrun the marines.

Man for man, the marines could then (and can still) point to the fact that there is no better conventional fighting force in the world. The six thousand men at Khe Sanh were more than ready, but if General Giap chose, he probably could have overwhelmed them with enough troops that no defense, no fire superiority, could have denied them. Had he decided to do so, General Giap would first have had to eliminate the hilltop marine outposts. Without them and without Lang Vei, Khe Sanh would have been in great peril.

If, as at Dien Bien Phu, the loss of life had been inconsequential to him, Giap could have used tactics similar to those of that battle. He possibly could have committed enough troops to first overwhelm the hilltops, dig his trenches close to the Khe Sanh defenses, and overwhelm them. Given enough time, artillery, and antiaircraft artillery, Giap could theoretically have delivered enough counterbattery artillery fire on the fire bases of Camp Carroll and the Rockpile to neutralize their support of Khe Sanh's defense. As at Dien Bien Phu, the weather could also have limited the effectiveness of air support.

. . .

A CAREFUL study of the battle reports from Lang Vei, of the tactical and strategic situations, and of the terrain of northernmost I Corps leads to the inevitable conclusion that any attempt to relieve Lang Vei, once the tank attack commenced, would have been an exercise in futility. The rescuers would have suffered an unacceptable level of casualties.

Other questions about the battle may never be answered. It is indeed strange, for example, that the NVA allowed the survivors of Lang Vei to pass safely through to Old Lang Vei, for the most part. This retinue included one speeding, bouncing jeep loaded with Green Berets from the TOC. And were the Green Berets at Lang Vei sacrificial lambs, dangled in front of the marines at Khe Sanh and the MIKE Force from Da Nang that only reached as far as Quang Tri? Why did the NVA stop their assault against Captain Willoughby's TOC? Did they want the Green Berets trapped in the bunker to continue to broadcast pleas for assistance, having targeted the relief forces from Khe Sanh or Da Nang?

If any relief force had reached Lang Vei and rescued the imperiled defenders there, would they not then have had to turn around and fight their way back? Was this not a replay of a number of similar rescue attempts and corresponding ambushes that the French had experienced in the First Indochina War? If the MIKE Force from Da Nang had been able to arrive in time, would their rescue attempt only have served to put 150 more men in an untenable situation? Would the same have been true of the marines? Would the rescue forces, in other words, perhaps have been additional cannon fodder for the NVA mill?

General Westmoreland had made every effort to see that Khe Sanh did not turn into another Dien Bien Phu, as President Johnson feared. Johnson was so afraid of such an event that he had his Joint Chiefs of Staff give him written guarantees that Khe Sanh would not fall to the enemy.

The marines, unlike the French at Dien Bien Phu, held the high ground surrounding the combat base. They had supporting fire from the 175mm guns at the fire bases of the Rockpile and Camp Carroll. Unfortunately, the attempt in August 1967 to deliver a battery of the 175mm guns to Khe Sanh had been foiled. As a result, the gunners at Khe Sanh could never effectively silence the NVA 130mm and 152mm guns shooting at them from inside Laos. Also, the 175s from Camp Carroll and the Rockpile were too far away from Lang Vei to lend assistance to the Green Berets.

The interservice rivalry between the Green Berets and the marines received much attention during the Second Indochina War. There always has been and probably always will be friendly rivalry between the elite units. The debate as to which unit is better can sometimes erupt into barroom brawls or other such conventional methods of proving a point. It is another matter entirely to lend credence to notions that the marines intentionally disregarded the request for a rescue mission. The men at Lang Vei had no idea what was happening at Khe Sanh, nor did they know what the marine staff officers there expected to happen at any moment.

The arguments between General Westmoreland and marine General Robert E. Cushman are no secret. Details are available in Robert Pisor's thoroughly researched book *The End of the Line*, as well as in John Prados and Ray Stubbe's *Valley of Decision*. General Westmoreland has presented his views in *A Soldier Reports*. Suffice it to say that Westmoreland felt that the marines constantly underestimated the strength of the enemy. He also felt that Cushman's planning for the use of the reinforcements the latter received before the Tet Offensive did not meet his expectations, and he took issue with Cushman's refusal to turn over the command of any aircraft not engaged in close air support of marines in combat. Westmoreland wanted them under the operational control of the air force at MACV headquarters.

General Cushman refused to turn over operational control because he knew that the request meant that marine air would be directed to any existing targets, whether or not they were in support of his marines. The intended mission of close air support for marine infantry and installations would disappear. Cushman knew that the reason marines did not have the heavy-artillery capability of similar-sized army units was that they could always depend upon marine air to make up the difference. This air capability allowed them more mobility by their not having to worry about transporting heavy artillery to battle areas.

The marines also had limited support of naval gunfire to assist them, but they had to be in range of the ships at sea. Additionally, every marine aviator had to have training as an infantryman so that they would know exactly what their gravel-crunching fellow marines were facing. When a marine officer called in an air strike immediately in front of his position in a tough combat situation, he knew that his men had better duck. If they did not, they would feel the heat of the jet wash from the Marine Corps aircraft as it came in so low over them that they could salute the pilot. An old homily for newly commissioned marine second lieutenants at the Basic School in Quantico, Virginia, was that you could tell the difference between the married pilots and the bachelors who were flying close air support. The carefree bachelors flew in under the telephone wires.

Cushman had seen his fellow marine at Westmoreland's headquarters, General Chaisson, reprimand air force general "Spike" Momyer. Chaisson felt that the 7th Air Force had not properly supported the marines at the Battle of Con Thien some months earlier. General Cushman refused to turn over operational control of his aircraft to Westmoreland, and he went over the general's head to Admiral Sharp in Hawaii. Sharp backed up Cushman, raising the hackles on the back of Westmoreland's neck when he sent ComUSMACV a telegram on 18 January 1968, suggesting that Westmoreland shelve his request for Marine Corps air assets.

Another example of a decision by the marine command at Khe Sanh not to send a rescue force for an embattled and exposed unit occurred in the battle for Khe Sanh village. Marine Lieutenant Thomas B. Stamper and his small civic-action detachment were under heavy attack by the NVA. This coincided with the Khe Sanh ammo-dump explosion early in the morning of 21 January 1968. Stamper radioed Colonel Lownds at the Khe Sanh Marine Corps combat base for help. The situation facing Lownds was disastrous, and he felt that the circumstances prevented him from immediately sending a relief force to evacuate the Khe Sanh village defenders.

Lownds did, however, provide Stamper with artillery and mortar fire support, which helped the imperiled marines to survive.

This was no easy task, as the ammo-dump supplies exploded from the intense heat. The marines firing the fire-support missions into Khe Sanh village were themselves in danger from their own ammunition exploding around them. To make matters worse, the NVA were hurtling six-foot-long 122mm rockets weighing one hundred pounds each through the foggy morning sky into the marine combat base.

As the Khe Sanh marines struggled to contain the critical damage to their ammunition supplies, while protecting themselves from the incoming mail from NVA guns and mortars, Lieutenant Stamper was also busy. He and his men were rallying the South Vietnamese forces in the village, and miraculously they repelled the attack of the NVA.

The NVA regrouped and attacked again, later in the afternoon. Again, air and artillery support came to the rescue of Stamper and his men. By the time the defenders had again repulsed the NVA, Lownds decided it was time to withdraw Stamper and his marines. Ruling out the use of a ground relief column due to the certainty of ambushes awaiting them, Colonel Lownds sent helicopters in for the Americans. He would have to let the South Vietnamese find their own way to safety.

The point was clear. Lownds had risked the loss of his own marines in the village, knowing that an immediate attempt to rescue them could cause more relief-force casualties than the total number of men already at risk. It was equally clear that ultimately, most of the indigenous forces were on their own. These were tough decisions, but that is why colonels receive more pay than privates—it is a lonely responsibility. The staff is there to advise and inform, but the final decision has to be made by the one wearing the eagles on the collar.

The Stamper situation was very similar to that of the Green Berets at Lang Vei. Colonel Lownds had specific orders to be ready to rescue or reinforce the Green Berets at Lang Vei with two rifle companies, either by ground or by helicopter assault. Lownds had the cards stacked against him. He knew that NVA armor had penetrated the camp at Lang Vei and that the camp probably could not hold out for long. Most of the Green Berets became trapped in the TOC.

Helicopters faced certain destruction, as their landing zones surely held awaiting tanks. Route 9 certainly had one ambush after another, just waiting for the relief force. His was a difficult choice, but, when he considered all the aspects, it was clear-cut. He just could not spare two rifle companies to assist the embattled Green Berets at Lang Vei, even though their officers begged to go. Lownds made the tough call, and not even Westmoreland would overrule his commander on the scene.

The Joint Chiefs of Staff had guaranteed a very-worried president that Khe Sanh would not fall. Johnson did not want and would not tolerate another Dien Bien

Phu, and Colonel Lownds did not intend to be the commander who let down his commander in chief. His marines would hold, come hell, high water, or General Giap himself.

The other relief force earmarked for the Lang Vei compound was another MIKE Force company at Da Nang, commanded by Maj. Adam Husar, the MIKE Force battalion commander. A radio call from Schungel awakened Husar just after 0200. Lang Vei had tanks on the CP (command post), and Schungel was ordering him to send in the MIKE Force. At that time of the early morning during the Tet holidays, such a move was no small order. Husar had to do some quick recruiting. It was almost a rogue's gallery composed of Chinese Nungs, Rhade montagnards, some former Viet Cong called Chieu Hoi, two Australians, and three Americans besides himself. The major quickly loaded his men into trucks and headed for the air base. The mixed bag of armed ethnic troops with diverse uniforms presented a problem in just obtaining entrance to the air base at that tense time. The Tet Offensive had everyone jumpy.

The original plan was for this quickly assembled force to fly directly into Khe Sanh from Da Nang. As they loaded the C-130, 3d Marine Amphibious Force notified Khe Sanh at 0335 that they would be arriving shortly. Unfortunately, Khe Sanh was absorbing its largest shelling to date, and its runway closed to large planes until later that morning. The planned dawn assault could not take place in the planned manner.

Thus, as the red sun rose over the South China Sea on 7 February, Husar's MIKE Force company of some

150 men was en route to Quang Tri aboard the C-130. Quang Tri was the closest place to Lang Vei that the C-130 could land. There they hoped to get enough helicopters to traverse the remaining ninety miles to Lang Vei and vertical-assault their way into a whale of a firefight.

By the time Husar's MIKE Force landed at Quang Tri, it was nearly 0600. Lang Vei, for all practical purposes, was already under the control of the enemy, at least above ground. Now only the legendary assaults led by Sergeant First Class Ashley still contested the outcome, and those would cease shortly after 1100. Unfortunately, there were no helicopters waiting for the MIKE Force at Quang Tri. There were none available. Major Husar, furious, vented his anger toward anyone he thought could help, all to no avail.

A frustrated MIKE Force battalion commander and his equally frustrated mercenaries returned to Da Nang that evening. Had the timing been perfect, they might have made a difference in the outcome. However, the number of lives they would have saved at that late hour would probably have been much fewer than those expended in the attempt.

THE U.S. Army's vaunted Flying Horsemen, the First Air Cavalry Division, embarked on Operation Pegasus and headed for Khe Sanh on 1 April 1968. When the First Cav arrived two weeks later, it marked the end of the Battle of Khe Sanh. Whether it had indeed been a siege in the strictest military meaning of the word remains a matter for debate.

The marines did not see Pegasus as a rescue mission. They had never met a massed enemy head on, in the manner that Westmoreland had planned in his hopes to annihilate several NVA divisions in a conventional war. Neither had it been necessary to send replacements for the gaunt and tired Leathernecks who had, for some seventy-seven days, withstood earth-shaking pounding from the sky. The rank-and-file marines were glad to leave the rats that had gnawed at their toes and fingers while they tried to sleep. However, they still had not had the opportunity to prove their mettle against the regular infantry divisions of General Giap at Khe Sanh, so their relief was a mixed blessing.

At the camp at Lang Vei, the First Air Cav found no survivors, only burned-out hulks of NVA tanks and trucks and the normal remnants of such a battle. For years there were unfounded rumors that the superstitious Bru would never return to the site of Lang Vei. Another rumor had it that the First Air Cav found something on the Lang Vei battlefield they had not seen before in the war: more than six hundred unburied corpses supposedly covered the battle scene, and the First Air Cav did not even stay the night. Lang Vei was a spooky place; it is easy to imagine it haunted by the souls of those who died locked in mortal combat there.

THE BATTLE of Lang Vei was significant enough that the what-ifs have continued for decades already. What if someone else had manned the 106mm recoilless rifle that normally would have been assigned to the young lieutenant on an authorized absence during the battle? As we have seen, Captain Willoughby and Lieutenants Longgrear and Wilkins disagree on whether or not anyone actually manned the second 106mm recoilless rifle during the battle. It may indeed have been manned for a short time—not long enough, or without enough ammunition. Willoughby says that he believes that all six beehive rounds were with the 106mm operated by Holt.

Would that single weapon have stopped the tanks coming from the direction of Laos and attacking the 102 and 103 Companies on the western perimeter? Would that have been enough to stop at least one penetration and perhaps swing the tide of battle? Would more antitank and beehive ammunition for the 106s have made the critical difference?

What if the marines had responded as directed? What if the artillery from Khe Sanh had commenced firing immediately, instead of seventeen minutes after the request? What if the MIKE Force at Da Nang had been able to obtain helicopters at Quang Tri? What if the 175mm guns had arrived safely at Khe Sanh the previous summer and been able to provide effective counterbattery fire against the NVA guns firing at them from Laos? What if the round had missed the marine ammunition dump at Khe Sanh? What if General Westmoreland had overruled Colonel Lownds? What if a platoon of Lieutenant Longgrear's MIKE Force had been on an OP south of the camp overlooking the trail to Lang Troai, where the first tanks attacked? What if the Laotian Royal Elephant Battalion commander had allowed his troops to help Ashley and the other Green Berets stage their counterattacks before dawn, as they had pleaded with him to do? What if the Green Berets could have laced their protective wire with antitank mines? What if the LAWs had not been air-dropped and were normally functional?

What if any combination of the above had been favorable to Special Forces Team A-101, the MIKE Force, and the indigenous troops, and Lieutenant Colonel Schungel? Would General Giap have simply poured in more troops and tanks? Did he in fact have more troops and tanks in the area? Certainly he had some in reserve. Was Hue the real target in northern I Corps, and not Khe Sanh and Lang Vei?

One thing is clear: the Green Berets at Lang Vei, as well as the MIKE Force and CIDG, did everything expected of them, and more. Of the twenty-four Green Berets, all but Sfc. James Holt (who was already missing in action) and Sgt. Richard Allen became wounded in action.

The eight Green Berets recommended by the Board of Inquiry to continue as missing in action became reduced by three during Operation Homecoming in 1973. The NVA had captured Sfc. Harvey G. Brande and S.Sgt. Dennis L. Thompson during the battle. On 18 February, just eleven days after being captured, they escaped. Somehow they were able to make their way back to the abandoned camp, where they hoped to find help. Brande, more seriously wounded than Thompson, was unable to continue on to the Marine Corps base at Khe Sanh. He ordered Thompson to leave him and save himself, but Thompson stayed with his fellow Green Beret. The NVA recaptured them within a few hundred meters of Lang Vei. Sp4c. William G. McMurry had also been captured, and he returned with Brande and Thompson in 1973, along with Sp4c. John Young, part of the group that had been sent to care for the Laotians, captured while on patrol on 30 January 1968.

When Sfc. James Holt had gone to look for more ammunition for his 106mm recoilless rifle, the Green Berets had never again seen him alive.

Sfc. Charles Lindewald and Sfc. Kenneth Hanna had been with the MIKE Force at the OP when the battle had begun. Lindewald had taken severe abdominal wounds, as reported by Dinh Chep, MIKE Force platoon leader. He had not seen Hanna wounded, but he had watched as Hanna and the radio operator carried Lindewald into the bunker at the OP. He then had seen a tank roll up to the wire and fire at the bunker, destroying it (and presumably killing Lindewald, Hanna, and the radio operator) and the machine gun behind it. Sergeant Hanna had reported to Captain Willoughby during the battle for the OP that fire from an automatic weapon had hit Lindewald in the chest.

Author David Stockwell in *Tanks in the Wire* reported Sfc. Earl Burke to have escaped to Old Lang Vei and assisted in the counterattacks led by Ashley. Unfortunately Burke's remains, found on Operation Pegasus, confirm his official status as killed in action on 7 February 1968. The First Air Cavalry recovered Ashley's remains as well.

Team sergeant Bill Craig was the last Green Beret to see Sp5c. Daniel R. Phillips alive. Craig saw Phillips with another Green Beret, probably Burke but perhaps

Holt. At the time, they were trying to E and E (escape and evade the enemy) through the outer wire, under fire from a tank that Craig feels was missing them.

It is unlikely that either Lindewald or Hanna survived the destruction of their bunker on the OP, but stranger things have happened. Lieutenant Colonel Schungel did not believe that McMurry could have survived, but he lived through five years in North Vietnamese prison camps. None of the four returning prisoners of war ever saw any of the other five, nor did they hear of them being in captivity.

10

PFOD (Write Off)

The method that the armed forces uses to account for
the change in status between missing in action and deceased is called a presumptive finding of death, or
PFOD. The provisions of Sections 555 and 556, Title
37, United States Code, authorize this action, which
provides an orderly transition to acceptance of what
most people would term the inevitable. The above Sections allow the secretary of the army, in the case of any
soldier, to delegate responsibility to a designated sub-
ordinate to declare a person presumed dead. Sections
551 through 554 of Title 37, United States Code, give
more background and purposes for such an event.

On 16 February 1968, a Western Union telegram arrived at the home of Mrs. Betsy Phillips, the widowed
mother of Sp5c. Daniel R. Phillips.

The adjutant general of the army, Maj. Gen. Kenneth G. Wickham, notified Betsy Phillips of the secretary of the army's deep regret that her son Daniel had
been missing in action since 7 February 1968. It informed her that when last seen, he had been on perimeter defense while his camp at Lang Vei was receiving

hostile mortar fire. It said that a search was in progress, and that the delay in notifying her was due to the tactical situation existing in Vietnam for the past few days. Mrs. Phillips received assurances of prompt advice when further information became available. The army asked for her cooperation by making public only information concerning her son's name, rank, service number, and date of birth. The telegram confirmed that she would have a personal visit from a representative of the secretary of the army, who would inform her of the facts regarding her son's status.

On 24 February, Mrs. Phillips received a follow-up telegram from the adjutant general, informing her that no additional information regarding her son was available. It informed her that the search for her son was continuing. It explained that, in those instances where a member of the armed forces' fate was indefinite, the circumstances surrounding the disappearance were subject to thorough investigation. She received information about the Board of Inquiry procedure, including the fact that the board could recommend, should there be sufficient evidence, that her son's status be changed to deceased. In the absence of adequately conclusive evidence that would support such a change in status, however, he would remain classified as missing in action. The telegram promised a follow-up during April 1968.

April brought nothing new. The months of her son's absence grew into years. Letters of comfort came periodically from the adjutant general, Maj. Gen. Verne L. Bowers.

On 11 August 1971, Betsy Phillips received word

that her missing son had received a promotion to the rank of staff sergeant.

In March 1973, the Paris peace talks finally resulted in the release of the American prisoners of war. Unfortunately, Daniel Phillips was not among them. Betsy Phillips had corresponded with his team sergeant, Bill Craig. Craig now gave her the names of four team members who might have knowledge of her son's fate or whereabouts.

She recognized the name of Dennis Thompson, as the television cameras showed him departing the plane at Clark Air Force Base on the Philippine Islands. She wrote to Thompson but received a reply from Col. Donald S. Aines of the adjutant general's office on his behalf. Aines stated that Thompson did not wish to correspond with anyone at that time.

In a letter dated 30 March 1973, Major General Bowers informed Mrs. Phillips that he shared the joy of the families of the returned prisoners, but he also realized how their return must affect her. President Nixon had told the nation that the enemy had released all U.S. prisoners, but Bowers informed Mrs. Phillips that his office would continue to stay in touch with her, through her FSAO (the family services assistance officer) as well as through his own office. Enclosed with the letter was Department of the Army Pamphlet 600-34, entitled *Handbook for the Next of Kin of Army Prisoners of War/Missing Personnel.* Its purpose was to provide answers to questions often asked by families of those still considered missing in action. The most frequently asked question was, obviously: How and when will the missing cases be resolved?

Mrs. Phillips learned that before any decision was made, all available data would again be subject to thorough and complete review and careful evaluation. All new sources of information, including the debriefing statements of returned prisoners, were subject to analysis. The Joint Casualty Resolution Center (JCRC) had the task of continuing the investigations into the status of those still missing and applying their findings to the data already on hand in each case. The JCRC would have its Southeast Asia base in Nakhon Phanom, Thailand. Its mission was the securing of information regarding missing U.S. personnel, and identifying remains at crash and grave sites.

Once the JCRC had satisfied itself that all the available information was in place, with no prospects for further data, it would consolidate and reassemble the pieces. This database would then interface with each unresolved case. With this type of operation, no time frame could be set. The task would be onerous and time-consuming, and more than likely it would take an extended period. Because of this seemingly indefinite and complex methodology, it was not expected that status changes would necessarily be held up until the JCRC had completed its work. Instead, each case would be judged on its own merits. A determination would follow as to whether the analysis was exhaustive enough to ascertain that there was little or no hope of any further information ever being uncovered on the case. A hot line exclusively for the next of kin of the missing came into use.

Major General Bowers wrote again on 27 August 1973, reporting on the Fourth Annual Convention of the National League of Families, held in Washington, D.C., from 26 to 29 July. This meeting provided a forum where the families could meet with government officials and ask questions to them directly. The head of the JCRC, Brig. Gen. Robert C. Kingston, who commanded the U.S. JCRC in Nakhon Phanom, Thailand, attended. He briefed the families on the difficulties that his organization was encountering, including the problem of properly identifying recovered remains, and the obstacles caused by the rough terrain. State Department and Department of Defense officials were also present.

Brigadier General Kingston assured the families that he and his staff were dedicated to their task and recognized the magnitude and importance of their assigned mission. He had experts in the fields necessary to do the job, and his personnel continued to make every effort to obtain the most complete information available to resolve open cases.

Major General Bowers said that a determination of death would occur only when the circumstances were such that there was no reasonable presumption that a serviceman could have survived. This statement represented a change from the time before the release of the returned prisoners. The army had hoped at that time to obtain some firsthand information from possible eyewitnesses or from anyone who might have had direct knowledge of the fate of some of the missing.

One significant—and negative—factor gleaned from the debriefings of the returned American prisoners of war was the fact that if no one had seen or heard of a particular person being held captive, it was unlikely they were still alive. Even prisoners who had been held in solitary confinement had developed their own secret communication system. Information, hope, and inspiration had passed from one prisoner to another, often at great risk.

Dan Phillips was one of those whose names went unreported by the returning prisoners, including those with whom he had only served at Lang Vei for three weeks or less: Thompson, Brande, and McMurry. What did this mean? It seemed strange, but Holt and Phillips had seemingly disappeared without a trace.

Holt appears to be the first to have disappeared. Had the NVA killed them and hauled their bodies away? Only God and a few NVA knew. Dan Phillips received a Category 1 MIA classification—the North Vietnamese had certain knowledge of his fate.

Because of the anxieties raised by classifying the missing into categories, the military discontinued this procedure. But regardless of procedure, there was, of course, a difference in the odds of finding a missing person shot down over a large body of water and finding a soldier who had been part of a force overwhelmed on the ground. The army had first used such reasoning to reach PFOD on six men lost over large bodies of water.

Bowers explained that a change in status from MIA to PFOD did not depend solely on the inspection of combat, grave, and crash sites, or on the recovery of remains. Instead, the determination depended upon a thorough review of all the available data. The intent was to continue the search for the remains to ascertain the cause of death, if possible. This was the stated responsibility of the Department of Defense to both the missing and their families. There would be no blanket determinations.

The adjutant general finished his letter by reiterating the obvious: the circumstances under which some men had disappeared, as well as the difficult terrain and the time elapsed since the incident, all compound the enigma. Bowers's people might never be able to recreate the complete circumstances of some of the men's disappearances. He was coordinating the efforts of his staff and those of the JCRC in Thailand by sending a staff member to headquarters there to expedite the dissemination of information to the families.

In a letter dated 16 November 1973, Major General Bowers mentioned the numerous inquiries his office was receiving regarding the recent initiation of a legal action. Because the matter was already in litigation, he could not comment on it. He enclosed a copy of that portion of the court order dated 6 August 1973 that placed restraints on the armed services in making changes of status except under certain conditions.

On 30 January 1974, Major General Bowers wrote to tell Mrs. Phillips that since the signing of the Paris agreement, seventy-seven American army prisoners of war had gained their freedom. He hoped for the recovery of the remains of many of our men believed to be dead but whose bodies were still undiscovered.

The results of that search had been disappointing. Over 90 percent of the reported battle or crash sites remained inaccessible to the efforts of the JCRC. This was due to the disagreement between the government of South Vietnam and the Provisional Revolutionary

Government (the Viet Cong) regarding control over the areas in question. The North Vietnamese government added to this frustration by failing to turn over the remains of air force personnel after showing their alleged grave sites to observers the previous May.

The JCRC had completed its work in those few crash sites in South Vietnam where the two opposing governments could agree to allow access. The JCRC continued to try to obtain access to additional sites in South Vietnam and Laos but would not attempt additional ground searches pending approval from both governments.

On 15 December 1973, unarmed Capt. Richard M. Rees and one South Vietnamese member of a JCRC search team were killed by hostile action while on an approved mission. The U.S. government sent a strongly worded diplomatic protest note to the chairman of the International Commission for Control and Supervision. This temporary cessation of ground searches would not result in the disbanding of the JCRC. The JCRC had just experienced a change in command due to the normal rotation of General Kingston back to the United States. His replacement was Brig. Gen. Joseph R. Ulatoski. It was Ulatoski's plan to resume the searches as soon as possible.

On 12 March 1974, Major General Bowers informed Mrs. Phillips of the status of the litigation regarding the case that became known as *McDonald v. McLucas*. He had alerted the families of those missing in action regarding the pending litigation on 16 November 1973. The subject of the case concerned the statutes known as the Missing Persons Act under Title

37 of the United States Code, Sections 555 and 556. A three-judge panel from the U.S. District Court for the Southern District of New York had heard the case on 23 October 1973 and had filed its opinion on 13 February 1974. The case had challenged the law's constitutionality concerning the procedures that the military departments used to review the cases of and effect the change in status of missing servicemen.

The panel of judges determined that the statute as written was contrary to law. Their reasoning was that it did not require the notification of the next of kin before a review of the missing serviceman's case could be undertaken. Such a review could result in the change in status from missing to deceased, but there was no avenue provided for the next of kin to participate and express their views in the case. The panel delivered its decision that the next of kin must receive proper notification of a pending review, have an opportunity to be present, and have counsel present at the review.

Before entering the final decree, the court expressed its mood. The adjutant general would allow no further action on cases concerning a change in status until the court had entered the formal decree and the legal interpretations were available. He anticipated only a brief delay. (As it turned out, the delay extended beyond expectations. The status review for those missing in action in Southeast Asia resumed in late August 1977.)

A letter from Major General Bowers on 27 February 1975 told Mrs. Phillips that the previous year had shown little progress toward the accounting required by the agreement concerning those missing. Both the government of North Vietnam and the Viet Cong provisional government refused to cooperate with the U.S. representatives in an effort to resolve the situation. Major General Bowers reported that forty of the seventy-seven returned army prisoners of war had remained on active duty. The army was helping the others adjust to civilian life.

The general expressed his concerns about families of the missing making their ways to Southeast Asia in search of information. He gently warned that past trips had yielded no meaningful information from the North Vietnamese, Viet Cong, or Pathet Lao. In fact, the North Vietnamese continued to refuse visas to the families of those still listed as missing in action. He also told the recipients of his letter that the U.S. embassies had essentially the same information as had already been furnished to the next of kin. He asked that these circumstances be fully considered before making travel commitments to the area.

The JCRC moved from Nakhon Phanom's Royal Thai Air Force Base to Samae San on 20 January 1975 and then to U Tapao on 9 February 1976. The number of personnel decreased from 160 to 105, while the mission and capabilities of the unit remained unchanged. The reduction in manpower and the relocation would have no effect on the intent of the Department of Defense to provide a complete accounting of the missing.

Major General Bowers reported that the fifth and final exchange of prisoners from Laos had taken place on 7 November 1974. The total included 217 Thai and 138 Royal Laotian government personnel. The JCRC queried these returnees to determine if they had any helpful information. The results were negligible, and the families concerned received whatever information was obtained.

The last letter from Major General Bowers was dated 29 August 1975. He was retiring from active service on 1 September and was reporting on the Sixth Annual Convention of the National League of Families, held in Washington on 18–20 July. Its highlight had been the appearance of President Ford the day before the convention had officially convened.

The president spoke to some family members as well as to the elected officials of the National League of Families. Ford reiterated his concern about and full support for obtaining an honorable accounting, and he would utilize all channels available to him. He also told his audience that there was no consideration of diplomatic recognition of North Vietnam, the former South Vietnam (the south was by now also ruled by the communists) or Cambodia. Perhaps most important, he stated categorically that reparations were "out of the question."

Shortly before the outgoing adjutant general wrote this last letter, some members of the U.S. House of Representatives had sent a letter to Pham Van Dong, the premier of North Vietnam. The letter concerned the open question of accounting for those still missing. The news media published the text of Pham Van Dong's reply, which laid out the specific conditions and provisions that were necessary for the exchange of information on those listed as missing in action. The families concerned received copies of his text.

Major General Bowers enclosed this with his letter to Mrs. Phillips. In closing, he introduced Maj. Gen. Paul Smith as his successor as adjutant general.

At the National League of Families convention, President Ford had mentioned Congress's interest in establishing a select committee to study the POW/MIA situation. Col. C. J. Bobinski, director of Casualty and Memorial Affairs, wrote to Betsy Phillips Hallam (who had remarried on 5 October 1974). He informed her that the House had passed a bill (HR 335) on 11 September 1975. The bill gave the select committee a broad mandate to conduct a thorough investigation of U.S. personnel still listed as missing in action. It would also include those killed in action, but whose bodies had not been recovered (KIA/BNR). The committee, chaired by Mississippi Democratic Congressman G. V. "Sonny" Montgomery, possessed full powers of subpoena. The committee would have a year to submit its report to the Congress.

Colonel Bobinski wrote again on 22 February 1976, reporting that the House Select Committee had met with President Ford on 17 December 1975. They had given the president a briefing on their talks with the Vietnamese diplomats in Paris. Chairman Montgomery had told President Ford about their continuing efforts to secure an accounting of the missing, as well as about the thoughts the committee had received from North Vietnamese ambassador Vo Van Sung. The ambassador had expressed his views on the normalization of relations, the lifting of the embargo on trade, and the need for humanitarian aid.

The committee had met with other Democratic Republic of Vietnam and Provisional Revolutionary Government officials to obtain more information on the missing. The Vietnamese had assured them they would carry out the promises they had made in the Paris agreements. They did not miss the opportunity to reiterate the obligation of the United States to help them rebuild their war-torn countries.

Lt. Col. Herman S. Marmon, U.S. Army, the assigned Family Services Assistance officer, called on Betsy Phillips Hallam at her home on 23 August 1977. He briefed her on the resumption of the status review of those missing in action in Southeast Asia. Her son had been missing for over nine and a half years, with no positive information ever received. She had never given up hope, but the chances of her ever seeing him alive again seemed to diminish with each passing day. She asked that when the time came that the army decided to review her son's status, Lieutenant Colonel Marmon notify her in person, and not by letter. She chose not to have legal counsel at the hearing, but she wanted Marmon to attend the review-of-status hearing with her.

Next she received a letter from Col. W. J. Winter, Jr., the director of Personal Affairs. Dated 15 February 1978, it stated that under the provisions of the Missing Persons Act, Title 37, United States Code, the secretary of the army was ready to review the casualty status of her son. Under army regulation 600-10, the secretary had to inform her of her rights:

1. She was to receive advance notice of the pending review, which the delivery of the letter accomplished.
2. She was given a reasonable opportunity to attend the hearing.

3. She had the right to have an attorney attend the hearing with her, but that would be at her own expense.
4. She would be provided reasonable access to the information on which the status review was based.
5. She would be afforded the opportunity to present any information that she considered relevant to the determination of status.

Betsy Phillips Hallam could, if she so desired, waive any or all the above rights. She elected to attend the hearing with Lieutenant Colonel Marmon.

On 18 May 1978, she and Lieutenant Colonel Marmon attended the hearing in Washington, D.C., which reviewed the MIA status of her son, S.Sgt. Daniel R. Phillips. The army furnished Mrs. Hallam with an itemized statement of the account that had been set up for her son at Fort Benjamin Harrison. His pay had continued for the ten years he had been considered missing in action. She learned of her son's selection for promotion to sergeant first class, the seventh enlisted grade, and that if the findings declared him deceased, he would receive a posthumous promotion.

Finally, the army informed Mrs. Hallam that should Danie Phillips be transferred to the PFOD status, she would receive any awards and decorations that her son had earned. The hearing adjourned just twenty-five minutes after it had begun.

A duly appointed hearing board composed of five members then decided the fate of Daniel R. Phillips. The reasoning for their decision to recommend a

PFOD was logical, if not simplistic: if we have not heard from or about him in more than ten years, he must be dead. On 19 July 1978, Col. W. J. Winter, Jr., the director of Personal Affairs for the adjutant general, forwarded the decision memorandum to the secretary of the army for his signature. Enclosed was a letter of condolence to Betsy Phillips Hallam.

The decision memorandum's purpose was to obtain the adjutant general's approval for a status change on S.Sgt. Daniel R. Phillips. The status would change from missing in action to a presumptive finding of death. The letter stated that the primary next of kin, Betsy Phillips Hallam, informed of the hearing officer's recommendation of the change in status, had delivered no response to the army. The official date of death would be listed as 10 July 1978. In essence the U.S. Army was writing S.Sgt. Daniel Phillips off in its books, and he was not alone. The U.S. government also wrote off all the other missing servicemen, with one exception. An air force colonel, Charles Shelton, was the only man not categorized PFOD, even though the 1991 edition of the Department of Defense's *POW-MIA Fact Book* states that intelligence reports indicate Shelton died in captivity in the mid-1960s. He stands as a symbol for those written off by their government. For reasons unknown, he continues to be classified as missing in action.

Postscript

The United States Army expressed its thanks for a job well done during the Battle of Lang Vei. Every one of the Special Forces present received an award for valor. All told, the twenty-four Green Berets received one Medal of Honor, one Distinguished Service Cross, nineteen Silver Stars, and three Bronze Stars with Combat V. The rescue force from MACV-SOG at FOB-3 received recognition for their heroism with one Distinguished Service Cross, two Silver Stars, seven Bronze Stars with Combat V, and two army Commendation Medals with Combat V. The list of awards for valor (with the men of the extraction force designated by an asterisk) is as follows:

6–7 FEBRUARY 1968, LANG VEI SPECIAL FORCES CAMP

Award of the Medal of Honor

For conspicuous gallantry and intrepidity in connection with military operations involving conflict with an armed hostile force in the Republic of Vietnam:

Detachment A-101, 5th Special Forces Group (Airborne), 1st Special Forces:

Ashley, Eugene, Jr., Sfc. E7 (posthumous).

Award of the Distinguished Service Cross

For extraordinary heroism in connection with military operations involving conflict with an armed hostile force in the Republic of Vietnam:

Company C, 5th Special Forces Group (Airborne), 1st Special Forces:

Schungel, Daniel F., Lt. Col. Inf.

Command and Control Detachment, Headquarters and Headquarters Company, 5th Special Forces Group (Airborne), 1st Special Forces:

*Quamo, George, Maj. Inf.

Award of the Silver Star

For gallantry in action while engaged in military operations involving conflict with an armed hostile force in the Republic of Vietnam:

Detachment A-101, 5th Special Forces Group (Airborne), 1st Special Forces:

Willoughby, Frank C., Capt. Inf.
Wilkins, Miles R., 1st Lt. Inf.
Craig, William T., Sfc. E7
Hanna, Kenneth, Sfc. E7 (missing in action)
Holt, James W., Sfc. E7 (missing in action)
Brooks, Arthur, S.Sgt. E6
Thompson, Dennis L., S.Sgt. E6 (captured,
repatriated)
Tiroch, Peter, S.Sgt. E6
Allen, Richard H., Sgt. E5
Fragos, Nickolas, Sgt. E5
Phillips, Daniel R., Sp5c. E5
(missing in action)
Johnson, Joel, Sp4c. E4

**Company C, 5th Special Forces Group (Airborne),
1st Special Forces:**

McMurry, William G., Sp4c. E4 (captured,
repatriated)

**Detachment A-113, 12th MSF CO, Mobile Strike
Force, Company C, 5th Special Forces Group
(Airborne), 1st Special Forces:**

Longgrear, Paul R., 1st Lt. Inf.
Brande, Harvey G., Sfc. E7 (captured, repatriated)
Lindewald, Charles W., Sfc. E7 (missing in action)
Burke, Earl F., Sfc. E7 (posthumous)
Early, John D., Sgt. E5 (missing in action)
Moreland, James L., Sp4c. E4 (missing in action)

Command and Control Detachment, Headquarters and Headquarters Company, 5th Special Forces Group (Airborne), 1st Special Forces:

*Secor, Gilbert, Sfc. E7
*Mullowney, Richard D., Sgt. E5

Award of the Bronze Star with V Device

For heroism in connection with military operations against a hostile force in the Republic of Vietnam:

Detachment A-101, 5th Special Forces Group (Airborne), 1st Special Forces:

Phillips, Emanuel E., S.Sgt. E6
Dooms, Franklin H., Sp4c. E4

Company C, 5th Special Forces Group (Airborne), 1st Special Forces:

Todd, Thomas E., 1st Lt. Engr.

Command and Control Detachment, Headquarters and Headquarters Company, 5th Special Forces Group (Airborne), 1st Special Forces:

*Fleming, Allen, 1st Lt. Inf.
*Pegram, Richard E., Com. Sgt. Maj. E9
*Cavanaugh, Robert L., Sfc. E7
*Cryan, Kenneth M., Sp5c. E5
*Harris, William M., Sp5c. E5

*Kirk, Stephen T., Sgt. E5
*Earley, Thomas S., Sp4c. E4

Several others in the rescue force from FOB-3 received army Commendation Medals with Combat V: M.Sgt. Charles J. "Skip" Minnicks; S.Sgt. John J. Allen, Jr.; and S.Sgt. Gary L. Seaburg.

The South Vietnamese government also presented the Vietnamese Cross of Gallantry with Bronze Palm to several of the Green Berets, including Captain Willoughby, First Lieutenant Longgrear, Sergeant First Class Craig, Staff Sergeant Tiroch, S.Sgt. Emanuel Phillips, and Staff Sergeant Brooks. (Several others may also have received the award.)

The commanding general of the 3d Marine Amphibious Force, Lt. Gen. Robert E. Cushman, Jr., awarded the twenty-four Green Berets of Lang Vei the U.S. Navy–Marine Corps Presidential Unit Citation for their actions during the battle.

This is the unit award that is given for heroism equal to the nation's second-highest award for bravery. The Navy Cross, the Air Force Cross, and the Army's Distinguished Service Medal are the individual equivalents of this decoration. Such cross-service recognition is an uncommon occurrence and signifies the importance placed on the contribution of the Lang Vei defenders to the Marine Corps combat base at nearby Khe Sanh.

LT. COL. Daniel Schungel and Capt. Frank Willoughby flew from Khe Sanh to Da Nang, where they entered the U.S. Naval Hospital for treatment of their multiple wounds. Even though they were in the same hospital, during that time they never saw each other or spoke about the battle. Schungel received a visit from two of his Company C officers: his adjutant, Capt. Edward T. Damaso, and his surgeon, Capt. Alan F. Hunter. Schungel saw no reason to recuperate in a naval hospital when he had his own medical facility nearby. Wearing Damaso's cap and Hunter's field jacket over his hospital gown, he walked out of the hospital between his two officers, both considerably larger than he. Although the navy raised a storm of protest, Schungel weathered it well.

He returned to duty after recovering from his wounds and again assumed command of Company C, 5th Special Forces Group (Airborne), 1st Special Forces, Da Nang. He extended his Vietnam tour for six months and finally returned stateside in November 1968, when he was promoted to colonel. The next month Schungel assumed command of the 7th Special Forces Group at Fort Bragg.

In February 1970, Schungel reported to Command and Control North, MACV-SOG. This tour lasted one year, after which Colonel Schungel returned to paperwork at the Pentagon for two years, serving under an air force general. Next he became the commander of the little-known Alternate National Military Command Center outside Fort Ritchie, Maryland. This super-secret underground facility provides, as its name suggests, an alternate command center in case of enemy attack. Its facilities are said to be impervious to atomic blasts, and army personnel sometimes refer to it simply as "the site."

After training national-guard troops in Saudi Arabia for a year, Schungel's final tour of duty before retirement was at Fort Ritchie as post commander. He retired in August 1978 to a large eighteenth-century farmhouse he had purchased some years before near Newville, Pennsylvania, and did much of the restoration himself. Daniel Schungel died in July 1990, and his widow still resides in southern Pennsylvania.

WILLOUGHBY SPENT approximately three weeks in the hospital, then returned to duty as the S-1 (adjutant) of Company C in Da Nang. One of his first duties was to interview Sgt. Richard Allen, who had recommended Sfc. Eugene Ashley, Jr., for the Medal of Honor. The news of Ashley's heroic exploits had spread quickly, even reaching Westmoreland's ear in Saigon. Willoughby believes that Colonel Ladd made the recommendation, based on Allen's report. Together, Willoughby and Schungel wrote the required background report for the army records.

Willoughby tried his best to escape the drudgery of commanding an LSD (large steel desk), but Lieutenant Colonel Schungel, still his commanding officer, denied Captain Willoughby that opportunity.

"You've been shot up enough," Willoughby remembers Schungel telling him. "You're a damned adjutant now. Stay here and push the papers." So Willoughby pushed the papers for five months, until he returned to the States for the Advanced Course. While waiting for his class to assemble, he was a "snowbird," in a standby status, so he served as a tactical officer for a West Point class starting Infantry Officers Basic Course.

Willoughby returned to Vietnam as the operations officer (S-3) of 2d Battalion, 506th Regiment (Airborne), 101st Airborne Division. In the ensuing eleven months and ten days, he would collect two more Purple Hearts. Originally scheduled to join his former company commander, Lt. Col. Daniel Schungel, at MACV-SOG, Willoughby was diverted to the 506th and was the only captain serving as an operations officer on that level in Vietnam.

He retired as a major in September 1978, after having served twenty-two years on active duty. Today Willoughby manages a farm and restores older houses in and around Phenix City, Alabama, where he lives.

First Lt. Paul Longgrear and Sfc. William T. Craig recuperated in a hospital in Japan. Longgrear then returned to the United States and completed his rehabilitation in the Fort Benning, Georgia, hospital in April 1968, with a newfound faith and the support of his family. Soon he returned to full duty as a company commander in the army training center at Fort Benning.

However, he knew he had to go back. Vietnam was where the action was, where the promotions came quickest, where life was a day-to-day, even a minute-by-minute experience. He called the Pentagon again, this time asking for reassignment to the 101st Airborne, the Screaming Eagles. He stopped by along the way to complete the army Ranger School.

Longgrear returned to Vietnam in August 1969 for a second tour, this time with the 23d Infantry "Americal" Division. When a major reported to the battalion for duty, Longgrear got the rifle-company command that he needed and wanted. In Vietnam, a key figure was the fatality rate inflicted upon the enemy: the body count. It was a game of numbers that started in the bush and wove its way through the various headquarters up the line, ending when the daily number found its way to Lyndon B. Johnson's breakfast table. Equally important numbers, of course, were the "friendly" losses: the number of Americans killed in action. Longgrear's brother-in-law, Freddy Jackson, became one of that number.

In January 1970, Longgrear served a tour as battalion executive officer. Next came a job as assistant operations officer of the brigade. Captain Longgrear completed his second tour in August 1970. He reported to the Armored Officers Advanced Course at Fort Knox, graduating in 1971. After earning his B.S. degree and serving a tour as an ROTC instructor in Florida, Longgrear served his final tour on active duty in Germany. He resigned his regular army commission in April 1976, maintaining a reserve commission until his retirement as a colonel after a total of twenty-eight years combined reserve and active duty service. Today Paul and Patty Longgrear run their own business in a small town not far from Atlanta. Longgrear, who in 1988 received an M.A. degree in Christian Counseling, preaches at a number of churches to fill in for vacationing ministers.

· · ·

FIRST LT. MILES Wilkins spent six weeks in hospitals in Japan and Da Nang. After recovery he assumed command of his own A-Team, also designated A-101, south of Dong Ha. Of the four years and three months he spent on active duty, Wilkins served twenty-eight months in Vietnam, from August 1967 until December 1969. He now lives with his family in a small town in Wisconsin, not far from the Mississippi River.

SFC. WILLIAM T. Craig spent three months recuperating from his wounds in hospitals in Japan. During his recuperation, he received his promotion to master sergeant. In January 1971, he returned to Vietnam in IV Corps for a year, serving in Chi Lang and training Cambodians. Two years later he received his final promotion to command sergeant major, the highest enlisted rank.

Bill Craig finally took off his jump boots after a career that had made him a legend in the Special Forces. He retired in November 1976. He has written several books.

AFTER SURVIVING the Battle of Lang Vei without a wound, Sgt. Richard H. Allen, who had tried valiantly to save his friend Sfc. Eugene Ashley, Jr., returned to duty. Along with Emanuel Phillips and Franklin Dooms, he soon found himself in a Marine Corps outpost called Hill 52. The three had jumped from the frying pan into the fire, as they discovered when fifteen hundred NVA surrounded their small unit and placed it under siege for about thirty days before a battalion of marines came to their rescue.

After the war, Rich Allen received an accounting degree and later an M.B.A. He has made a career in accounting and finance and lives in Southern California.

Notes on Sources

Prelude

The background of the four Green Berets was provided by numerous personal interviews and correspondence with Frank C. Willoughby, Paul R. Longgrear, and William T. Craig. Daniel R. Phillips is my first cousin, and his background was provided by personal interviews with his mother—Betsy Phillips Hallam—and by his personal papers, which she so graciously gave to me. The remainder of the prelude comes from my personal knowledge and experience. "The men we left behind" is taken from the title of the book by Mark Sauter and Jim Sanders, listed in the bibliography.

Chapter 1

A number of authors, including key participants, have told the story of the U.S. Marines' defense of the combat base at Khe Sanh. However, in my opinion, two accounts stand out. Robert Pisor's *The End of the Line: The Siege of Khe Sanh* and the joint work of John Prados and navy chaplain Ray W. Stubbe, *Valley of Decision: The Siege of Khe Sanh,* are both very readable and filled with those personal glimpses that make the reader feel present at the siege. Those two works are the main references for the chapter. Regarding NVA tanks' main guns, I referred to Francis J. Kelly's *U.S. Army Special Forces, 1961–1971*, p. 110. Also important were interviews with Col. Frances J. "Blackjack" Kelly and then-Capt. Allan B. Imes.

Chapter 2

Information for this chapter comes primarily from Daniel Phillips's Army Personnel File, from interviews with Betsy Phillips Hallam, and from Daniel Phillips's high-school scrapbook, yearbook, and notes. Also important were interviews with the participant Green Berets, listed in the Interviews.

Chapter 3

The Green Beret who was a prime source for this chapter was then-lst. Lt. Paul R. Longgrear, commander of the MIKE Force at Lang Vei.

Also helpful were interviews with Mrs. Daniel F. Schungel, the widow of then-Lt. Col. Daniel F. Schungel, and the MIKE Force battalion commander, then-Maj. Adam Husar.

Chapter 4

There are many books about the Green Berets, the most famous of which is Shelby L. Stanton's *Green Berets at War: U.S. Army Special Forces in Southeast Asia, 1856–1975.* I found valuable information in James Adams's *Secret Armies* and in Bruce Quarrie's *Special Forces*.

No book, however, can take the place of talking to one or more of these finely honed fighting men. I was most fortunate in receiving unending cooperation from every one of the Green Berets I interviewed.

Chapters 5–7

The books consulted for the background for these chapters were primarily Prados and Stubbe's *Valley of Decision*, *Pisor's End of the Line* and David B. Stockwell's *Tanks in the Wire*, a book dedicated solely to the battle of Lang Vei during Tet, 1968. Captain Harrington's quotation on the scene looking like the Fourth of July (Chapter 6) comes from Stockwell's book, p. 127. Also in Chapter 6, Fragos's conversation with the NVA appeared originally in *Newsweek*, 19 February 1968, p. 42.

There are always confusing details following a battle: as after any exciting event, viewpoints can vary significantly. Also, no single Green Beret saw the entire battle. The outpost platoon of First Lieutenant Longgrear's MIKE Force became heavily engaged simultaneously with the CIDG 104 Company on the perimeter facing the trail from Lang Troai. The men trapped in the Tactical Operations Center could see very little of the battle. They were receiving radio reports from the entire camp, from the outpost, and from Khe Sanh, all at the same time. First Lt. Paul Longgrear experienced the tank attack outside the TOC, then went through the nightmare of being trapped within the TOC, and finally acted as the point for the escape from the TOC. Today, he credits a higher power for his survival. Interviews with him were not only informative, they were almost spellbinding.

The A-Team commanding officer, then-Capt. Frank Willoughby, and later his senior noncommissioned officer, then-Sfc. William Craig, oversaw the building of the Special

Forces camp. Willoughby's battle station was in the TOC, co-ordinating the defense of the camp by radio. He also dashed up the stairs (while they existed) to see as much as he could, in order to make adjustments to air and artillery support. The air support, incidentally, included an Arc Light B-52 bombing attack south of the camp near Lang Troai. The results of the attack are unknown, but it had to be devastating to the enemy. In our many lengthy interviews, Frank Willoughby presented a commander's view of a terrifying, tragic, and heroic defense, adding much new material to what has previously been published.

Craig saw the battle from the western perimeter of the camp and escaped through the wire. He then took part, although suffering from multiple wounds, in the heroic attempts to counterattack and free those trapped in the TOC. The information, constructive criticism, and advice from Bill "Pappy" Craig were essential to this writing.

As alternate next of kin to Daniel Phillips, I have had access to his service records and MIA file. His mother, Betsy Phillips Hallam, is primary next of kin and named me as the alternate to provide succession.

Additionally, two officers in charge of the Joint Casualty Resolution Center in Alexandria, Virginia—Lt. Col. James Cole and his successor, Lt. Col. Mack Brooks—showed interest and a keen desire to help. They consistently provided me with complete access to the records. With undermanned and overworked staffs, they did their best to satisfy the needs of so many MIA families.

Chapter 8

The primary sources for this chapter were personal interviews (listed in the Interviews section) with the participants as mentioned. The quotes from General Westmoreland's book *A Soldier Reports* are taken from pp. 341–45.

Chapter 9

Wherever later accounts of the battle differed in some respects from official reports, I used the official reports. However, I also allowed for the typographical errors that occur frequently in military correspondence and documents, especially in the names of the participants. Additionally, there have been minor instances in published accounts of the battle where the authors have incorrectly identified participants at particular locations and actions. This is understandable, as the chaos and confusion that occurs in any firefight of this magnitude and duration can certainly wreak havoc with the memories of even the most involved and combat-experienced soldiers. Another drawback to the accuracy of identification was that much of the fighting took place during the hours of darkness. Illumination was primarily by sporadic, eerie light provided by airborne flares from Spooky, supported by artillery and mortar illumination shells.

It is entirely possible that later recollections of the participants might vary from their earlier official reports and statements. The passage of time sometimes improves accuracy, but it can also adversely influence the observations of a party to the action. The opinions expressed in this chapter are my own. Many of them are reflected in the books already listed above; many were derived from interviews with participants.

Chapter 10

This chapter's source is the MIA file of Daniel Phillips.

Postscript

The awards and decorations are listed in official U.S. Army records, orders, and documents. Announcement of Awards, TC 320 Dept. of the Army, Headquarters, USAVN, APO San Francisco 96375. Personal information originated from interviews as listed in the Interviews section.

Bibliography

Published Sources

Adams, James. *Secret Armies*. New York: Atlantic Monthly Press, 1987.

Albright, John, John A. Cash, and Allan W. Sandstrum. *Seven Fire Fights in Vietnam*. Washington, D.C.: Office of the Chief of Military History, United States Army, 1970.

Bonds, Ray. *The Vietnam War*. New York: Military Press, 1988.

Caputo, Philip J. A. *Rumor of War*. Toronto: Holt, Rinehart and Winston, 1977.

Colby, William. *Lost Victory*. Chicago: Contemporary Books, 1989.

Corson, William R. *The Betrayal*. New York: Norton, 1968.

Craig, William T. *Lifer!* New York: Ivy Books, 1994.

Craig, William T., Sgt. Maj. "Armored Assault on Lang Vei." *Vietnam*, February 1995.

Currey, Cecil B. *Edward Lansdale: The Unquiet American*. Boston: Houghton Mifflin, 1988.

Davidson, Phillip B. *Vietnam at War*. Novato, Calif.: Presidio Press, 1988.

Department of the Army. *After Action Report: Battle of*

Lang Vei. Company C, 5th Special Forces Group (Airborne), 1st Special Forces, APO San Francisco, 1968.

Department of the Army, Headquarters. *A Field Manual of Guerrilla Warfare and Special Forces Operations*, FM 31-21, September 1961.

Department of the Army, Headquarters. *Special Forces Handbook*. ST 31-180.

Department of Defense. *POW-MIA Fact Book*. July 1991.

Devillers, Philippe, and Jean Lacouture. *End of a War*. New York: Praeger, 1969.

Donahue, Jeffrey C. *Indochina POW Timeline*. Privately published, distributed by the Connecticut chapter, National Forget-Me-Not Association for POW/MIAs. February 1990.

Donovan, Robert J. *Nemesis*. New York: St. Martin's Press, 1984.

Fall, Bernard. *Hell in a Very Small Place*. New York: Lippincott, 1966.

Ferguson, Ernest B. *Westmoreland*. Boston: Little, Brown and Co., 1968.

Gettleman, Marvin E. *Vietnam: History, Documents and Opinions*. New York: Mentor, 1970.

Samuel B. Griffith, trans. *Mao Tse-tung on Guerrilla Warfare*. New York: Praeger, 1961.

"How the U.S. Lost Lang Vei." *Newsweek*, 19 February 1968.

Huyen, N. Khac. *Vision Accomplished? The Enigma of Ho Chi Minh*. New York: Macmillan, 1971.

Isaacson, Walter. *Kissinger*. New York: Simon and Schuster, 1992.

Johnson, Lyndon Baines. *The Vantage Point: Perspectives of* the Presidency, 1963–1969. New York: Holt, Rinehart and Winston, 1971.

Kahin, George McTurnan, and John W. Lewis. *The United States in Vietnam*. N.p.: Delta, 1967.

Karnow, Stanley. *Vietnam: A History*. New York: Viking Press, 1983.

Kelly, Francis J. *U.S. Army Special Forces, 1961–1971*. Vietnam Studies series. Washington, D.C.: Department of the Army, 1973.

Kutler, Stanley I., ed. *Encyclopedia of the Vietnam War*. New York: Charles Scribner's Sons, 1996.

Lacouture, Jean. *Ho Chi Minh*. New York: Random House, 1968.

Lanning, Michael L. and Dan Cragg. *Inside the VC and the NVA*. New York: Fawcett Columbine, 1992.

Lehrack, Otto J. *No Shining Armor: The Marines at War in Vietnam*. Lawrence, Kans.: University Press of Kansas, 1992.

Macdonald, Peter. *Giap*. New York: W. W. Norton, 1993.

Neumann-Hoditz, Reinhold. *Portrait of Ho Chi Minh*. New York: Herder and Herder, 1972.

Olson, James S. *The Vietnam War: Handbook of the Literature and Research*. Westport, Conn.: Greenwood, 1993.

O'Neill, Robert J. *General Giap: Politician and Strategist*. New York: Praeger, 1969.

Phillips, William R. "The Magnificent Sacrifice." *Behind the Lines,* September–October 1996.

Pisor, Robert. *The End of the Line: The Siege of Khe Sanh*. New York: W. W. Norton, 1982.

Prados, John, and Ray W. Stubbe. *Valley of Decision: The Siege of Khe Sanh*. Boston: Houghton Mifflin, 1991.

Quarrie, Bruce. *Special Forces.* Secaucus, N.J.: Chartwell, 1990.

Rust, William J. *Kennedy in Vietnam.* New York: Charles Scribner's Sons, 1985.

Sauter, Mark, and Jim Sanders. *The Men We Left Behind.* Washington, D.C.: National Press, 1993.

Schurmann, Franz, Peter Dale Scott, and Reginald Zelnik. *The Politics of Escalation in Vietnam.* Greenwich, Conn.: Fawcett, 1966.

Sigler, David Burns. *Vietnam Battle Chronology: U.S. Army and Marine Corps Combat Operations, 1965–1973.* Jefferson, N.C.: McFarland, 1992.

Simpson, Charles M., III. *Inside the Green Berets.* Novato, Calif.: Presidio Press, 1983.

Stockwell, David B. *Tanks in the Wire.* Canton, Ohio: Daring, 1989.

Summers, Harry G., Jr. *Vietnam War Almanac.* New York: Facts on File Publications, 1985.

———. *Historical Atlas of the Vietnam War.* Boston: Houghton Mifflin, 1995.

Turley, William S. *The Second Indochina War.* New York: Mentor, 1987.

U.S. Senate. *Report of the Select Committee on POW/MIA Affairs,* Report 103-1, 13 January 1993.

U.S. Senate Committee on Foreign Relations. *An Examination of U.S. Policy Toward POW/MIAs.* Republican staff, release date 23 May 1991.

U.S. Senate Committee on Foreign Relations. *Interim Report on the Southeast Asian POW/MIA Issue.* Republican staff, release date 29 October 1990.

Vetter, Lawrence C. *Never Without Heroes.* New York: Ivy Books, 1996.

Westmoreland, Gen. William C. *A Soldier Reports*. New York: Da Capo, 1989.

Wise, David, and Thomas B. Ross. *The Invisible Government*. New York: Random House, 1964.

Zaloga, Steven J., and James W. Loop. *Soviet Tanks and Combat Vehicles*. New York: Sterling, 1987.

Unpublished Sources

Ladd, Jonathan F., Col., U.S. Army Special Forces (Ret.). Transcript of an oral history interview conducted 26 February 1977 by Col. James R. Bergan, U.S. Army, and Lt. Col. Willard M. Burleson, U.S. Army. Creighton Abrams Oral History Project papers, Archives, U.S. Army Military History Institute, Carlisle Barracks, PA 17013.

Longgrear, Paul R. Letters. November 1967–February 1968.

Schungel, Daniel F. Lt. Col., U.S. Army Special Forces (Ret.). Transcript of an oral history interview conducted in 1988 by G. A. Hoskins. Senior Officer Oral History Program, Educational Services Division, U.S. Army Military History Institute, Carlisle Barracks, PA 17013.

Shulimson, Jack, and Maj. Leonard A. Blasiol. *1968 U.S. Marines in Vietnam,* Chapter 14. Forthcoming.

Interviews

Allen, Richard A., formerly Sgt., U.S. Army Special Forces.

Berg, Charles, formerly S.Sgt., U.S. Army Special Forces (Military Assistance Command Vietnam, Studies and Observation Group, Forward Operating Base Three).

Brooks, Mack, Lt. Col., U.S. Army (Ret.).

Cavanaugh, Robert L., formerly Sfc., U.S. Army Special Forces (Military Assistance Command Vietnam, Studies and Observation Group, Forward Operating Base Three).

Cole, James, Lt. Col., U.S. Army (Ret.).

Cottrell, Max, formerly Capt., U.S. Army Special Forces.

Cowperthwait, William, Lt. Col., U.S. Marine Corps (Ret.).

Craig, William T., Com. Sgt. Maj. (formerly Sfc.), U.S. Army Special Forces (Ret.).

Damaso, Edward T., Maj. (formerly Capt.), U.S. Army Special Forces (Ret.).

Fleming, Allen, formerly 1st Lt., U.S. Army Special Forces (Military Assistance Command Vietnam, Studies and Observation Group, Forward Operating Base One).

Hallam, Betsy Phillips, mother of Daniel R. Phillips.

Hoch, Kurt, Lt. Col., U.S. Marine Corps (Ret.).

Husar, Adam, Lt. Col. (formerly Maj.), U.S. Army Special Forces (Ret.).

Imes, Allan B., Lt Col. (formerly Capt.), U.S. Army Special Forces (Ret.).

Kelly, Francis J., Col., U.S. Army Special Forces (Ret.).

Longgrear, Paul R., Col. (formerly 1st Lt., U.S. Army Special Forces), U.S. Army Reserve (Ret.).

Lownds, David, Col., U.S. Marine Corps (Ret.).

McLeroy, James, formerly 1st Lt., U.S. Army Special Forces.

Minnicks, Charles J., Com. Sgt. Maj. (formerly M.Sgt.), U.S. Army Special Forces (Ret.).

Mullowney, Richard D., Jr., formerly Sgt., U.S. Army Special Forces.

Peck, Millard A., Col., U.S. Army (Ret.). Formerly head of POW/MIA Section, Defense Intelligence Agency.

Schlatter, Joseph A., Col., U.S. Army. Formerly head of POW/MIA Section, Defense Intelligence Agency.

Schungel, Mrs. Daniel F., widow of Lt. Col. Daniel F. Schungel, U.S. Army Special Forces (Ret.).

Sherman, Steve, formerly 1st Lt., U.S. Army Special Forces.

Smith, David C., Col., U.S. Army Special Forces (Ret.).

Westmoreland, William C., Gen., U.S. Army (Ret.).

Wilkins, Miles R., formerly 1st Lt., U.S. Army Special Forces. Later promoted to Capt.

Wilkinson, James B., Col. (formerly Lt. Col.), U.S. Marine Corps (Ret.).

Willoughby, Frank C., Maj. (formerly Capt.), U.S. Army Special Forces (Ret.).

Index